CONTENTS

CRISPY MUSSEL PANCAKES

Yield: Servings 2–4

INGREDIENTS:

- ¼ cup all-purpose flour
- ¼ teaspoon salt
- ½ cup tapioca flour
- ¾ cup water
- 1 cup shelled mussels (approximately 1 pound before shelling)
- 1 teaspoon baking powder
- 2 cups bean sprouts
- 2 tablespoons chopped cilantro, plus extra for decoration
- Salt and ground pepper to taste

DIRECTIONS:

1. To prepare the mussels, wash them swiftly using cool running water. Debeard the mussels by pulling out the brown membrane that is sometimes still attached. Discard any mussels that are already open. Fill a big frying pan with ½ to an inch of water. Bring the water to its boiling point, then put in the mussels, cover, and allow to steam approximately four minutes or until the mussels have opened, shaking the pan every so frequently. Drain the mussels through a colander. Allow to cool to room temperature and then use a small fork to pull the meat from the shell; set aside using paper towels.

2. In a moderate-sized-sized mixing container, mix together the flours, the salt, and the baking powder. Whisk in the water to make a thin batter.

3. Preheat your oven to 200 degrees. In a large, heavy-bottomed frying pan, heat the vegetable oil on moderate to high heat. Pour half of the batter into the frying pan and top with half of the mussels. Cook until the batter has set and turned golden, approximately 2 minutes. Cautiously flip the pancake over and carry on cooking until golden. Take away the pancake to a baking sheet lined with some foil and place it in your oven to keep warm. Repeat to make a second pancake with the rest of the batter and mussels.

4. Put in 1 teaspoon of vegetable oil to the frying pan if it is dry, and raise the heat to high. Put in the bean sprouts, drizzle with salt and ground pepper to taste, and stir-fry swiftly just to heat through, approximately half a minute.

5. To serve, place each pancake in the middle of a plate. Top with the bean sprouts, some cilantro, and a grind of fresh pepper. Serve with a sweet-and-sour sauce of your choice.

CURRIED FISH CAKES

Yield: 15–20 small cakes

INGREDIENTS:

- ¼ cup chopped garlic
- ¼ cup chopped lemongrass, inner portion only
- ¼ cup chopped shallots
- ½ pound French beans, trimmed and finely chopped
- ½ tablespoon salt
- ½ teaspoon peppercorns
- 1 egg, beaten
- 1 pound boneless whitefish steak, minced
- 1 tablespoon chopped ginger
- 1 tablespoon shrimp paste
- 1 teaspoon grated lime peel
- 5–10 dried chilies, seeded, soaked, and shredded
- Vegetable oil for frying

DIRECTIONS:

1. Put the shallots, garlic, lemongrass, ginger, peppercorns, lime peel, shrimp paste, chilies, and salt in a food processor or blender and process to make a smooth paste.
2. Put in the fish to the food processor and pulse until well blended with the spice paste. Put in the beaten egg and mix one more time. Move the fish mixture to a big mixing container and mix in the green beans.
3. Using roughly 1 tablespoon of fish mixture, form a flat, round cake; repeat until all of the mixture is used.
4. Heat roughly to ¼ inch of vegetable oil to 350 degrees on moderate to high heat in a frying pan or deep fryer; fry the fish cakes until golden.
5. Serve with a dipping sauce of your choice.

FRIED TOFU WITH DIPPING SAUCES

Yield: Servings 2–4

INGREDIENTS:

- 1 package of tofu, cut into bite-sized cubes
- Dipping sauces of your choice
- Vegetable oil for frying

DIRECTIONS:

1. Put in approximately two to three inches of vegetable oil to a deep fryer or wok. Heat the oil on medium until it reaches about 350 degrees. Cautiously add some of the tofu pieces, ensuring not to overcrowd them; fry until a golden-brown colour is achieved, turning continuously. Move the fried tofu to paper towels to drain as each batch is cooked.

2. Serve the tofu with a choice of dipping sauces, such as Sweet-and- Sour, Peanut, and Minty Dipping Sauce .

DILL RICE

Yield: Servings 2–4

INGREDIENTS:

- 1 cup long-grained rice (such as Jasmine)
- 1 green chili pepper, seeded and minced
- 1½ cups water
- 2 green cardamom pods
- 2 tablespoons vegetable oil
- 4 tablespoons chopped fresh dill
- Salt

DIRECTIONS:

1. In a moderate-sized-sized pot, heat the vegetable oil on moderate heat. Put in the cardamom pods and sauté for a minute. Put in the chili and sautée. for a short period of time. Mix in the salt and the dill and cook for another two to three minutes. Put in the rice and sauté for 3 more minutes.

2. Mix in the water and bring the mixture to its boiling point. Decrease the heat, cover, and simmer for twenty to twenty-five minutes or until the liquid has been absorbed.

3. Take away the cardamom pods and fluff the rice before you serve.

FAR EAST FRIED RICE

Yield: Servings 4–6

INGREDIENTS:

- ¼ cup chopped mint or cilantro leaves
- ¼ cup roasted peanuts, chopped
- 1 bunch green onions, trimmed and thinly cut
- 1 teaspoon dried red chili pepper flakes
- 1½ tablespoons rice vinegar
- 2 big carrots, peeled and crudely shredded
- 2 cups bean sprouts, trimmed if required
- 2 eggs, beaten
- 2 tablespoons fish sauce
- 2 tablespoons minced garlic
- 2 tablespoons sugar
- 2½ tablespoons vegetable oil
- 5 cups day-old long-grain white rice, clumps broken up

DIRECTIONS:

1. Mix the fish sauce, rice vinegar, and sugar in a small container; set aside.
2. In a wok or big frying pan, heat the oil on moderate to high heat. Put in the eggs and stir-fry until scrambled.
3. Put in the green onions, garlic, and pepper flakes and continue to stir-fry for fifteen seconds or until aromatic.
4. Put in the carrots and bean sprouts; stir-fry until the carrots start to tenderize, approximately 2 minutes.
5. Put in the rice and cook for two to three minutes or until thoroughly heated.
6. Mix in the fish sauce mixture and put in the fried rice, tossing until uniformly coated.
7. To serve, decorate the rice with chopped mint, or cilantro, and chopped peanuts.

FLAVORFUL STEAMED RICE

Yield: Servings 2–4

INGREDIENTS:

- ¼ cup chicken or vegetable broth
- ½ cup finely chopped cilantro
- ¾ cup long-grained rice
- 1 tablespoon minced gingerroot
- 1 teaspoon fish sauce
- 1 teaspoon salt
- 2 cloves garlic, minced
- 2 green onions, trimmed and thinly cut
- 2 teaspoons lime juice

DIRECTIONS:

1. Bring a pot of water to a rolling boil. Put in the rice, allow the water to return to its boiling point, and cook for about ten minutes. Drain in a sieve, wash, and save for later. (Leave the rice in the sieve.)
2. Put in 1 inch of water to the pot and bring to its boiling point. Set the sieve over the boiling water, cover it using a clean kitchen towel and a lid, and allow to steam for approximately twenty minutes. (Check once in a while, putting in more water if required.)
3. Mash together the garlic and the salt to make a paste.
4. In a big container, mix the garlic paste, broth, gingerroot, green onions, lime juice, and fish sauce.
5. Put in the steamed rice and toss until well blended. Allow to cool to room temperature.
6. Mix the cilantro into the rice.

FRAGRANT BROWN RICE

Yield: Servings 4–6

INGREDIENTS:

- 1 cups brown rice (white rice can be substituted)

- 1 kaffir lime leaf or 2 (2-inch-long, -½inch-wide) pieces of lime zest
- 1 medium carrot, peeled and julienned
- 1 tablespoon finely chopped gingerroot
- 1 tablespoon lime juice
- 1½ stalks celery, trimmed and thinly cut
- 2 garlic cloves, minced
- 2 red chili peppers, seeded and minced
- 2 tablespoons vegetable oil
- 4 green onions, trimmed and thinly cut
- 4½–5½ cups vegetable stock
- Salt and freshly ground pepper to taste

DIRECTIONS:

1. In a moderate-sized to big deep cooking pan, heat the vegetable oil on medium. Put in the garlic and green onions, and cook for a couple of minutes. Put in the celery, carrots, chilies, and ginger, and cook for another two minutes.

2. Put in the rice and stir until well blended. Put in half of the vegetable stock, the kaffir lime leaf, lime juice, and salt and pepper. Bring to its boiling point; decrease the heat and simmer, uncovered, for fifty minutes, putting in additional stock as required.

PEANUT DIPPING SAUCE — 1

Yield: Approximately 2 cups

INGREDIENTS:

- ¼ cup chicken or vegetable stock
- ¼ cup heavy cream
- ¼ cup lemon juice
- 1 teaspoon grated gingerroot
- 1½ cups coconut milk
- 2 tablespoons brown sugar
- 2 tablespoons soy sauce

- 3–4 dashes (or to taste) Tabasco
- 4 cloves garlic, pressed
- 1 cup crispy peanut butter

DIRECTIONS:

1. Mix the peanut butter, coconut milk, lemon juice, soy sauce, brown sugar, ginger, garlic, and Tabasco in a small deep cooking pan on moderate heat. Cook while stirring continuously, until the sauce has the consistency of heavy cream, approximately fifteen minutes.
2. Move the mixture to a blender and purée for a short period of time.
3. Put in the stock and cream, and blend until the desired smoothness is achieved.

PEANUT DIPPING SAUCE — 2

Yield: Approximately 2 cups

INGREDIENTS:

- ¼ cup fresh lime juice
- ¼ cup half-and-half or heavy cream
- ¼ cup low-sodium beef broth
- 1 teaspoon grated gingerroot
- 1½ cups unsweetened canned coconut milk
- 2 tablespoons brown sugar
- 2 tablespoons soy sauce
- 2 teaspoons minced garlic Ground cayenne or crushed red pepper flakes to taste
- 1 cup crispy peanut butter

DIRECTIONS:

1. In a moderate-sized-sized deep cooking pan, mix the peanut butter, coconut milk, lime juice, soy sauce, brown sugar, ginger, garlic, and cayenne.
2. Stirring continuously, cook on moderate heat until the sauce thickens, approximately fifteen minutes.
3. Take away the sauce from the heat and put in the beef broth and cream. Using a hand mixer, blend until the desired smoothness is achieved. Heat for a short period of time just prior to serving.

FRIED WON TONS

Yield: Approximately 25 won tons

INGREDIENTS:

- ½ cup chopped white mushrooms
- ½ pound ground pork
- 1 clove garlic, minced
- 1 tablespoon soy sauce
- 2 tablespoons minced cilantro
- 25 won ton skins
- Pinch white pepper
- Vegetable oil for frying

DIRECTIONS:

1. In a moderate-sized-sized mixing container, meticulously mix the garlic, cilantro, soy sauce, mushrooms, white pepper, and ground pork.
2. To make the won tons, place roughly ½ teaspoon of the filling in the center of a won ton skin. Fold the won ton from corner to corner, making a triangle. Push the edges together to secure closed. Repeat with the rest of the skins and filling.
3. Put in approximately two to three inches of vegetable oil to a deep fryer or wok. Heat the oil on medium until it reaches about 350 degrees. Cautiously add the won tons, 2 or 3 at a time. Fry until they become golden brown, turning them continuously. Move the cooked won tons to drain using paper towels as they are done.
4. Serve the won tons with either sweet-and-sour sauce or the sauce of your choice.

MEE KROB

Yield: Servings 4–6

INGREDIENTS:

- ½ cup dried shrimp
- ½ pound thin rice stick noodles, broken into handfuls

- 1 cup bean sprouts

- 1 tablespoon Tamarind Concentrate (Page 20)

- 10 small lime wedges

- 2 eggs, beaten

- 2–3 drops red food coloring

- 5 tablespoons sugar

- 1 cup honey

- 1 cup rice or white vinegar

- Vegetable oil for deep-frying

DIRECTIONS:

1. Mix the honey, vinegar, sugar, food coloring, and tamarind in a moderate-sized deep cooking pan. Bring the mixture to its boiling point on moderate heat, stirring once in a while. Decrease the heat and simmer for two to three minutes or until the mixture starts to thicken; turn off the heat and save for later.

2. Bring about 3 inches of vegetable oil to 360 degrees in a deep fryer or frying pan. Drop a single layer of the rice stick noodles into the hot oil, ensuring to leave enough room for them to cook uniformly. Turn the noodles using a slotted spoon the moment they start to puff up. Once the noodles are golden, remove them to paper towels to drain. Repeat until all of the noodles are cooked.

3. Put in the dried shrimp to the oil and cook for 45 seconds or so. Remove to paper towels.

4. Pour out all but a thin coat of the oil from the frying pan. Put in the beaten eggs and stir-fry them swiftly, shirring them into lengthy strips. Once they are cooked, remove them to paper towels.

5. Bring the sauce back to its boiling point. Mix in the shrimp and continue to boil for a couple of minutes.

6. Put about of the noodles on a serving platter and spoon about of the sauce over the top; lightly toss to coat the noodles uniformly being cautious not to crush the noodles. Repeat until all of the noodles are coated in sauce.

7. To serve, mound the noodles, put the egg strips over them, and top with the bean sprouts. Pass the lime wedges.

OMELET "EGG ROLLS"

Yield: 16–20 pieces

INGREDIENTS:

For the filling:

- ½ pound ground pork or chicken
- ½ teaspoon sugar
- 1 cup shredded Chinese cabbage
- 1 tablespoon fish sauce
- 1 tablespoon minced cilantro
- 1 teaspoon vegetable oil
- 2 green onions, trimmed and thinly cut

For the omelets:

- 1 tablespoon soy or fish sauce
- 1 teaspoon vegetable oil
- 6 tablespoons water
- 8 eggs
- Bibb lettuce
- Decorate of your choice
- Soy sauce, fish sauce, and/or hot sauce

DIRECTIONS:

1. To make the filling: In a moderate-sized-sized frying pan, warm the vegetable oil on moderate heat. Put in the ground meat and sauté until it is no longer pink. Put in the green onions and cabbage and cook until tender. Put in the sugar, fish sauce, and cilantro; cook for 1 more minute. Set the filling aside, keeping it warm.

2. To make the omelets: Mix the eggs, water, and soy sauce in a moderate-sized container. Put an omelet pan on moderate heat for a minute. Put in roughly ¼ teaspoon of vegetable oil, swirling it to coat the pan uniformly. Pour roughly ¼ of the egg mixture into the pan, then allow it to rest for roughly half a minute. When the bottom is firm, flip the omelet and cook until done. Transfer to a plate and cover using foil to keep warm. Repeat to make 3 more omelets.

3. To fill the "Egg Rolls," place 1 omelet in the middle of a plate. Put ¼ of the filling slightly off-center and then roll up. Trim the ends and chop the rolls into bite-sized pieces.

4. To serve, use Bibb lettuce leaves to pick up the rolls. Immerse in additional soy sauce, fish sauce, hot sauce, or other favorite dipping sauce, and put in the decorate of your choice.

PORK TOAST TRIANGLES

Yield: 24 pieces

INGREDIENTS:

- ¼ pound of big shrimp, peeled and deveined

- 1 egg

- 1 pound ground pork (the leaner the better)

- 1 tablespoon chopped cilantro

- 1 tablespoon dried shrimp

- 1 tablespoon fish sauce

- 2 cloves garlic, peeled

- 6 slices day-old bread, crusts trimmed off

- Vegetable oil for frying

DIRECTIONS:

1. Fill a moderate-sized deep cooking pan with water and bring it to its boiling point. Reduce the heat, put in the shrimp, and simmer until the shrimp are opaque. Drain the shrimp and let cool completely. Coarsely cut and save for later.

2. Put the dried shrimp, cilantro, and the garlic in a food processor and pulse until a smooth paste is formed. Put in the reserved shrimp and ground pork; process once more. Put in the egg and fish sauce and process one more time.

3. Spread the mixture uniformly over each slice of bread. Chop the bread into 4 equal slices, either from corner to corner forming triangles or from top to bottom forming squares.

4. Put in roughly ½ inch of vegetable oil to a big frying pan. Bring the oil to roughly 375 degrees on moderate to high heat. Put 4 to 5 toasts in the oil, filling side down. Ensure that the toasts are not crowded in the oil or they will not brown uniformly. After the filling side is well browned, use a slotted spoon or metal strainer to flip the toasts. Watch the toasts cautiously, as the bottoms will brown swiftly. Take away the toasts to a stack of paper towels to drain. Cautiously pat the tops of the toasts using paper towels to remove any oil.

5. Serve the toasts with sweet-and-sour or plum sauce.

PORK, CARROT, AND CELERY SPRING ROLLS

Yield: 20 rolls

INGREDIENTS:

- ¼ cup fish sauce
- ¼ teaspoon white pepper
- 1 cup bean sprouts
- 1 cup minced or ground pork
- 1 teaspoon minced garlic
- 2 cups chopped celery
- 2 cups grated carrots
- 2 egg yolks, beaten
- 2 tablespoons sugar
- 2 tablespoons vegetable oil
- 20 spring roll wrappers
- Vegetable oil for deep frying

DIRECTIONS:

1. In a big frying pan, heat the 2 tablespoons of vegetable oil over moderatehigh heat. Put in the garlic and pork, and sauté until the pork is thoroughly cooked.
2. Put in the carrots, celery, fish sauce, sugar, and white pepper. Increase heat to high and cook for a minute.
3. Drain any liquid from the pan and allow the mixture to cool completely, then mix in the bean sprouts.
4. On a clean, dry work surface, put the egg roll wrapper with an end pointing toward you, making a diamond. Put roughly 2 tablespoons of the filling on the lower portion of the wrapper. Fold up the corner nearest you and roll once, then fold in the sides. Brush the rest of the point with the egg yolk and finish rolling to secure. Repeat with the rest of the wrappers and filling.
5. Heat 2 to 3 inches of oil to 350 degrees. Deep-fry the spring rolls until a golden-brown colour is achieved; remove instantly to drain using paper towels.

6. Serve with sweet-and-sour sauce.

RICE PAPER ROLLS

Yield: Servings 2–4

INGREDIENTS:

- 1 cup thin rice noodles
- 4 (8″ × 10″) sheets of rice paper
- 1 cup grated carrot
- 2 scallions, thinly cut
- 1 small cucumber, shredded 20 mint leaves
- 1 small bunch cilantro
- 8–10 medium to big cooked shrimp, cut in half

DIRECTIONS:

1. Soak the rice noodles in super hot water until they are soft, usually ten to twenty minutes; drain. You can leave the noodles whole, or cut them into two-inch pieces if you prefer.
2. Put a sanitized kitchen towel on a work surface with a container of hot water nearby. Place a sheet of the rice paper in the hot water for roughly twenty seconds, just until soft; lay it out flat on the towel.
3. In the center of the rice paper, place 2 to 3 pieces of shrimp and ¼ of the noodles, carrots, scallions, and cucumbers. Top with mint and cilantro.
4. Swiftly roll up the rice paper, keeping it quite tight; then roll up the whole thing using plastic wrap, ensuring to keep it tight. Place in your fridge until ready to serve.
5. To serve, trim the ends off the rolls. Chop the remaining roll into pieces and remove the plastic wrap. Serve with a dipping sauce of your choice.

SALT-CURED EGGS

Yield: 1 dozen eggs

INGREDIENTS:

- 1 dozen eggs
- 1½ cups salt
- 6 cups water

DIRECTIONS:

1. Mix the water and the salt in a big deep cooking pan and bring to its boiling point using high heat. Turn off the heat and let cool completely.

2. Cautiously place the eggs in a container. Pour the salt water over the eggs and seal the container firmly. Put the container in your fridge and let the eggs cure for minimum 1 month.

3. To serve, hard-boil the eggs, let cool completely, then peel, slice, and enjoy.

SHRIMP TOAST

Yield: 32 pieces

INGREDIENTS:

- ¼ pound ground pork
- ¼ teaspoon salt
- ½ pound shrimp, cleaned, deveined, and crudely chopped
- 1 egg, beaten
- 1 tablespoon chopped cilantro
- 2 cloves garlic, minced
- 2 tablespoons sesame seeds
- 2 teaspoons soy sauce
- 2 teaspoons vegetable oil, divided
- 32 slices cucumber
- 8 slices of white bread, left to sit out overnight, crusts removed
- teaspoon cayenne

DIRECTIONS:

1. In a small container, mix the shrimp and pork; set aside.
2. In another small container, mix the cilantro, garlic, cayenne, and salt. Pour the spice mixture over the shrimp and pork, and combine.
3. Mix in the beaten egg and soy sauce; mix thoroughly. Split the mixture into 8 parts.
4. Smoothly spread a slim layer of the mixture on each slice of bread and drizzle with sesame seeds.

5. Heat ¼ teaspoon vegetable oil in nonstick frying pan. When it is super hot, place 1 piece of bread, meat side down, in the oil. Cook until golden in color, then remove to a paper towel, blotting any surplus oil. Repeat for all of the bread sides.

6. Cut each slice of bread into four equivalent portions and top each quarter with a cucumber slice.

SKEWERED THAI PORK

Yield: Servings 2–3

INGREDIENTS:

- 1 pound pork, thinly cut into lengthy strips
- 1 tablespoon coconut milk
- 1 tablespoon fish sauce
- 1 teaspoon salt
- 2 tablespoons sugar
- 20–30 bamboo skewers, soaked in water for an hour
- 3 cloves garlic, minced

DIRECTIONS:

1. In a moderate-sized-sized container, mix the sugar, salt, garlic, fish sauce, and coconut milk.
2. Toss the pork strips in the mixture to coat completely. Cover the container and marinate for minimum 30 minutes, but if possible overnight in your fridge.
3. Thread the pork strips onto the bamboo skewers.
4. Grill the skewers for approximately 3 to five minutes per side.
5. Serve with your favorite sauce or as is.

SON-IN-LAW EGGS

Yield: 20

INGREDIENTS:

- ¼ cup chopped cilantro
- ¼ cup vegetable oil

* 10 hard-boiled eggs, cooled and peeled
* 2 shallots, thinly cut
* 3 tablespoons fish sauce
* 1 cup light brown sugar
* 1 cup Tamarind Concentrate (Page 20)
* Dried hot chili flakes to taste

DIRECTIONS:

1. Heat the vegetable oil in a frying pan on moderate heat. Put the whole eggs in the frying pan and fry until a golden-brown colour is achieved. Take away the eggs to paper towels and save for later. (If your frying pan can't hold all of the eggs easily, do this in batches.)

2. Put in the shallots to the frying pan and sauté until just starting to brown. Take away the shallots from the oil using a slotted spoon and save for later.

3. Place the brown sugar, fish sauce, and tamarind in the frying pan. Stir to blend and bring to a simmer. Cook the mixture, stirring continuously, until the sauce thickens, approximately five minutes; turn off the heat.

4. Chop the eggs in half vertically and put them face-up on a rimmed serving dish. Spread the shallots over the eggs and then sprinkle the eggs with the sauce. Decorate using cilantro and chili pepper flakes.

SPICY COCONUT BUNDLES

Yield: Servings 4

INGREDIENTS:

* ½ cup chopped lime segments
* ½ cup chopped peanuts
* ½ cup diced red onion
* ½ cup dried shrimp
* 1 cup shredded fresh coconut
* 1–2 jalapeños, seeded and cut
* 20–25 moderate-sized spinach leaves, washed and patted dry
* 1 cup brown sugar
* 1 cup shrimp paste

DIRECTIONS:

1. Put the coconut in a moderate-sized sauté pan and cook on moderate heat until browned, approximately twenty minutes; allow to cool.

2. In a small deep cooking pan, melt the brown sugar on moderate heat, stirring continuously. Stir in the shrimp paste until well blended. Set the sauce aside.

3. Put the coconut, onion, lime pieces, peanuts, dried shrimp, and jalapeños in a moderate-sized serving container; lightly toss to blend.

4. To serve, place four to 5 spinach leaves (depending on the size of the leaves) on each serving plate. Top each leaf with roughly 1 tablespoon of the coconut mixture and sprinkle a small amount of sauce over the coconut.

5. To eat, roll up the spinach leaf around the coconut mixture and pop the whole bundle in your mouth. Pass additional sauce separately.

SPICY GROUND PORK IN BASIL LEAVES

Yield: Servings 4

INGREDIENTS:

*   ¼ tablespoon (or to taste) ground dried chili pepper
*   ½ pound ground pork
*   1 shallot, thinly cut
*   1 tablespoon toasted rice powder (available in Asian specialty stores)
*   3 tablespoons fish sauce
*   5 sprigs cilantro, chopped
*   Juice of 1–2 limes
*   Lettuce and/or big basil leaves

DIRECTIONS:

1. Squeeze the juice of half of a lime over the ground pork and let marinate for a few minutes.

2. Heat a big frying pan on high. Put in a couple of tablespoons of water and then instantly put in the pork; stir-fry until the pork is thoroughly cooked. (It is okay if the pork sticks at first — it will ultimately loosen.)

3. Pour off any fat that has collected in the pan and then put the pork in a big mixing container. Put in the remaining lime juice (to taste), fish sauce, shallot, ground chili pepper, cilantro, and toasted rice; stir until blended meticulously.

4. To serve, put the mixture in a serving container and let guests use the lettuce and basil leaves to scoop out the mixture.

SPICY SCALLOPS

Yield: Servings 4

INGREDIENTS:

- 1 (½-inch) piece of ginger, peeled and minced
- 1 clove garlic, minced
- 1 jalapeño, seeded and minced
- 1 teaspoon vegetable oil
- 2 tablespoons soy sauce
- 2 tablespoons water
- 8 big scallops, cleaned
- teaspoon ground coriander

DIRECTIONS:

1. In a pan big enough to hold all of the scallops, heat the oil on moderate heat. Put in the garlic, jalapeño, and ginger, and stir-fry for approximately one minute.

2. Put in the coriander, soy sauce, and water, stirring to blend; simmer for two to three minutes. Strain the liquid through a fine-mesh sieve. Allow the pan to cool slightly.

3. Put in the scallops to the pan and spoon the reserved liquid over the top of them. Return the pan to the stove, increasing the heat to moderate-high. Cover the pan and let the scallops steam for approximately two to three minutes, or until done to your preference. Serve instantly.

THAI FRIES

Yield: Servings 4–8

INGREDIENTS:

- 1 14-ounce bag shredded sweetened coconut

- 1 cup rice flour
- 1 cup sticky rice flour
- 1 pound taro root
- 1 teaspoon black pepper
- 1 teaspoon salt
- 2 moderate-sized sweet potatoes
- 2 tablespoons sugar
- 3 tablespoons black sesame seeds
- 4 green plantains
- Water

DIRECTIONS:

1. Peel the root vegetables and cut them into flat -inch-thick strips about 3 inches long and an inch wide.

2. Mix the flours in a big mixing container and mix in ½ cup of water. Continue putting in water ¼ cup at a time until a mixture resembling pancake batter is formed. Mix in rest of the ingredients.

3. Fill a moderate-sized deep cooking pan a third to a half full with vegetable oil. Heat the oil using high heat until super hot, but not smoking.

4. Put in some of the vegetables to the batter, coating them thoroughly. Using a slotted spoon or Asian strainer, put the vegetables in the hot oil. (Be careful here: The oil may spatter.) Fry the vegetables, turning them once in a while, until a golden-brown colour is achieved. Move the fried vegetables to a stack of paper towels to drain, then serve instantly.

ASIAN CHICKEN NOODLE SOUP

Yield: Servings 4 to 6

INGREDIENTS:

- ½ cup chopped onion
- 1 carrot, peeled and julienned
- 1 cup chopped cilantro
- 1 moderate-sized sweet red pepper, seeded and julienned
- 2 cups chicken broth

- 2 star anise

- 2 tablespoons chopped ginger

- 2 tablespoons fish sauce

- 2 tablespoons vegetable oil

- 2 whole boneless, skinless chicken breasts, cut into lengthy strips

- 3 cloves garlic, minced

- 3 ounces snow peas, trimmed

- 4 ounces, cellophane noodles, soaked in boiling water for five minutes and drained

- 5 cups water, divided

- Lemon or lime wedges

- Peanuts, crudely chopped

DIRECTIONS:

1. In a big deep cooking pan, heat the oil on high. Put in the onion and sauté until translucent. Put in the ginger, garlic, and cilantro, and sauté for 1 more minute. Mix in the broth and 2 cups of the water. Put in the star anise. Bring to its boiling point, reduce heat, and cover; simmer for twenty minutes to half an hour.

2. In another deep cooking pan, bring the rest of the water to its boiling point. Put in the vegetables and blanch for a minute or until soft-crisp. Drain and run very cold water over the vegetables to stop the cooking process; set aside.

3. Strain the broth into a clean soup pot and bring to its boiling point. Put in the chicken strips and reduce heat. Poach the chicken using low heat until opaque, roughly ten minutes. Put in the cellophane noodles and reserved vegetables, and carry on simmering for two more minutes. Season to taste with fish sauce.

4. To serve, ladle the soup into warm bowls. Drizzle with peanuts and decorate with lime wedge.

CHICKEN SOUP WITH LEMONGRASS

Yield: Servings 4–6

INGREDIENTS:

- ¾ pound boneless, skinless chicken breast, trimmed and slice into bite-sized pieces

- 1 (14-ounce) can unsweetened coconut milk

- 1 (1-inch) piece ginger, cut into 6 pieces

- 1 clove garlic, minced

- 1 medium onion, minced

- 1 stalk lemongrass, trimmed, bruised, and slice into 2 to 3 pieces

- 1 tablespoon vegetable oil

- 2 cups wild or domestic mushrooms, cut into bite-sized pieces (if required)

- 2 tablespoons fish sauce

- 2 teaspoons prepared Red Curry Paste (Page 17) or curry powder

- 3 lime leaves (fresh or dried)

- 4 cups chicken broth

- Juice of 2 limes

- Salt and pepper to taste

DIRECTIONS:

1. In a moderate-sized-sized deep cooking pan, mix the oil, onion, and garlic. Cook on moderate heat for a minute. Put in the lemongrass, curry paste, ginger, and lime leaves.
2. Cook while stirring, for about three minutes, then put in the broth. Bring to its boiling point, decrease the heat to moderate, and carry on cooking for ten more minutes.
3. Put in the coconut milk, the chicken pieces, and the mushrooms. Continue to cook for five minutes or until the chicken is done.
4. Mix in the lime juice and fish sauce. Sprinkle salt and pepper to taste.
5. Take away the lemongrass, lime leaves, and ginger pieces before you serve.

CHILLED MANGO SOUP

Yield: Servings 2–4

INGREDIENTS:

- 1 cup plain yogurt

- 1 tablespoon dry sherry

- 1 teaspoon sugar (not necessary)

- 1½ cups chilled chicken or vegetable broth

- 2 big mangoes, peeled, pitted, and chopped

- Salt and white pepper to taste

DIRECTIONS:

1. Put all of the ingredients in a blender or food processor and process until the desired smoothness is achieved. Adjust seasonings.
2. This soup may be served instantly or placed in the fridge until needed. If you do place in your fridge the soup, allow it to sit at room temperature for about ten minutes or so before you serve to take some of the chill off.

LEMONY CHICKEN SOUP

Yield: Servings 4–6

INGREDIENTS:

- ½ cup lemon slices, including peel
- 1 cup straw mushrooms
- 1 tablespoon minced fresh ginger
- 1 whole boneless, skinless chicken breast, poached and shredded
- 1½ cups coconut milk
- 1½ teaspoons fresh hot chili pepper, seeded and chopped
- 1½ teaspoons sugar
- 2 cups chicken broth
- 2 green onions, thinly cut
- 3 tablespoons fish sauce
- 3 teaspoons lemongrass, peeled and chopped

DIRECTIONS:

1. Mix the lemon slices, fish sauce, chili pepper, green onion, and sugar in a small glass container; set aside.
2. Mix the coconut milk, chicken broth, lemongrass, mushrooms, and ginger in a deep cooking pan. Bring to its boiling point, reduce heat, and simmer for twenty to twenty-five minutes. Put in the chicken and lemon mixture; heat through.

3. To serve, ladle into warmed bowls.

PUMPKIN SOUP

Yield: Servings 4

INGREDIENTS:

For the broth:

- 1 clove of garlic, halved
- 1 moderate-sized leek, cut
- 1 red chili pepper, cut in half and seeded
- 1 small banana, cut
- 1 small pumpkin, peeled, seeded, and cut into little chunks
- 1 tablespoon finely chopped ginger
- 1 tablespoon Green Curry Paste
- 1½ stalks celery, cut
- 2 tablespoons butter
- 3 stalks lemongrass, peeled and thinly cut
- 3¼ cups vegetable broth
- 1 cup coconut milk
- 1 cup half-and-half
- Salt and pepper to taste

For the chicken and vegetables:

- ¾ cup cooked rice
- 1 small Japanese eggplant, cut into 4 pieces
- 1 tablespoon vegetable oil
- 1 whole boneless, skinless chicken breast, trimmed and slice into strips
- 2 kaffir lime leaves, cut into strips
- 2 red chili peppers, cut in half and seeded (not necessary)
- 2 tablespoons butter
- 2 teaspoons finely chopped ginger

* 2 teaspoons prepared Green Curry Paste
* Thai basil

DIRECTIONS:

1. In a big pot, melt the butter on moderate heat. Put in the pumpkin, leeks, celery, bananas, chili pepper, lemongrass, garlic, and ginger; sweat for five minutes.

2. In another sauté pan, heat the vegetable oil. Put in the eggplant and sauté until just warmed through.

3. Melt the butter in a heavy-bottomed sauté pan on moderate heat. Put in the chicken strips, ginger, lime leaves, and curry paste. Sauté until the chicken is cooked, but not browned. Put in the chicken mixture to the broth.

4. Put in the half-and-half, coconut milk, and curry paste; simmer for fifteen to twenty minutes.

5. Put in the vegetable broth and heat until warm.

6. Take away the chili pepper halves. Move the broth mixture to a blender or food processor and purée until the desired smoothness is achieved. Strain if you wish, and season to taste with salt and pepper. Pour the mixture into a clean pot and keep warm. To prepare the chicken and vegetables:

7. To prepare the broth:

8. To serve, split the rice among 4 soup bowls. Ladle the broth over the rice. Top with a piece of eggplant, a chili pepper half (if you wish), and some basil.

SPICY SEAFOOD SOUP

Yield: Servings 4–6

INGREDIENTS:

* ¼ cup cut green onions
* 1 pound moderate-sized raw shrimp, peeled and deveined, shells reserved
* 1 quart water
* 1 tablespoon vegetable oil
* 10 (-inch-thick) slices fresh ginger
* 2 fresh serrano chilies, seeded and chopped
* 2 quarts fish or chicken stock
* 2 tablespoons fish sauce
* 2 tablespoons lime juice

- 24 fresh mussels, cleaned

- 3 stalks lemongrass, peeled and chopped

- 3 tablespoons chopped fresh cilantro

- 6–8 kaffir lime leaves

- Red pepper flakes to taste

- Salt

- Zest of 1 lime, grated

DIRECTIONS:

1. Heat the vegetable oil in a big deep cooking pan. Put in the shrimp shells and sauté until they turn bright pink. Put in the stock, water, lemongrass, lime zest, lime leaves, ginger, and serrano chilies. Bring to its boiling point, reduce heat, and simmer for half an hour Strain the broth into a clean soup pot.

2. Bring the broth to its boiling point. Put in the mussels, cover, and cook until the shells open, approximately 2 minutes. Use a slotted spoon to remove the mussels, discarding any that have not opened. Take away the top shell of each mussel and discard. Set aside the mussels on the half shell.

3. Put in the shrimp to the boiling broth and cook until they are opaque, approximately 2 minutes. Decrease the heat to low.

4. Put in the mussels to the pot. Mix in the lime juice, fish sauce, cilantro, red pepper flakes, and green onions. Simmer for one to two minutes. Season to taste with salt.

5. Serve instantly.

THAI-SPICED BEEF SOUP WITH RICE NOODLES

Yield: Servings 4–6

INGREDIENTS:

- ¼ cup fish sauce

- ¾ cup leftover beef roast, chopped or shredded

- 1 (2–inch) cinnamon stick

- 1 stalk lemongrass, tough outer leaves removed, inner core crushed and minced

- 1 tablespoon prepared chiligarlic sauce

- 1 whole star anise, crushed

- 2 (¼–inch) pieces peeled gingerroot

- 2½ tablespoons lime juice

- 3–4 teaspoons (or to taste) salt

- 8 cups beef broth

- 8 ounces rice noodles, soaked in hot water for approximately ten minutes, strained and washed in cold water

- Freshly ground black pepper to taste

DIRECTIONS:

1. In a moderate-sized-sized deep cooking pan, simmer the beef broth, star anise, cinnamon stick, and ginger using low heat for thirty to forty minutes.
2. Strain the stock and return to the deep cooking pan.
3. Put in the noodles, lemongrass, shredded beef, fish sauce, chili sauce, and garlic. Bring the soup to its boiling point on moderate heat. Decrease the heat and simmer for five minutes.
4. Mix in the lime juice, salt, and pepper.

TOM KA KAI

Yield: Servings 4–6

INGREDIENTS:

- 1 (1-inch) piece ginger, cut thinly

- 1 (2-inch) piece of lemongrass, bruised

- 1 boneless, skinless chicken breast, cut into bite-sized pieces

- 1 teaspoon cut kaffir lime leaves

- 2 cups chicken broth

- 2 tablespoons lime juice

- 2–4 Thai chilies (to taste), slightly crushed

- 4 tablespoons fish sauce

- 5 ounces coconut milk

DIRECTIONS:

1. In a moderate-sized-sized soup pot, heat the broth on medium. Put in the lime leaves, lemongrass, ginger, fish sauce, and lime juice.

2. Bring the mixture to its boiling point, put in the chicken and coconut milk, and bring to its boiling point once more.

3. Reduce the heat, put in the chilies, and cover; allow to simmer until the chicken is thoroughly cooked, approximately 3 to five minutes.

4. Take away the chilies and the lemongrass stalk using a slotted spoon before you serve.

TOM YUM

Yield: Servings 4–6

INGREDIENTS:

- 1 can straw mushrooms, drained
- 2 stalks lemongrass, bruised and slice into 1-inch-long segments
- 2 tablespoons fish sauce
- 2 tablespoons minced fresh ginger
- 20 moderate-sized shrimp, shelled but with tails left on
- 2–3 teaspoons cut kaffir lime leaves or lime zest
- 2–3 Thai chili peppers, seeded and minced
- 3 shallots, finely chopped
- 3 tablespoons lime juice
- 4–5 cups water

DIRECTIONS:

1. Pour the water into a moderate-sized soup pot. Put in the shallots, lemongrass, fish sauce, and ginger. Bring to its boiling point, reduce heat, and simmer for about three minutes.

2. Put in the shrimp and mushrooms, and cook until the shrimp turn pink. Mix in the lime zest, lime juice, and chili peppers.

3. Cover and take out of the heat. Allow the soup to steep for five to ten minutes before you serve.

VEGETARIAN LEMONGRASS SOUP

Yield: Servings 4–6

INGREDIENTS:

- ½ cup crudely shredded carrots
- ½ cup cut celery
- 1 can straw mushrooms, drained
- 1 cup snow peas, trimmed
- 1 red serrano chili, seeded and thinly cut
- 1 teaspoon (or to taste) crushed red peppers
- 4 tablespoons soy sauce
- 4–6 stalks lemongrass, bruised
- 8 cups low-sodium vegetable broth
- Juice of ½ lime or to taste

DIRECTIONS:

1. Bring the broth to a simmer in a big deep cooking pan. Put in the crushed red peppers, lemongrass, soy sauce, and lime juice. Simmer for about ten minutes.
2. Put in the rest of the ingredients. Continue to simmer until the vegetables are just done, approximately two to three minutes. Take away the lemongrass stalks before you serve.

ASIAN NOODLE AND VEGETABLE SALAD

Yield: Servings 4–6

INGREDIENTS:

- ¼ pound snow peas, trimmed and cut on the diagonal
- ½ cup toasted peanuts, chopped
- 1 cup bean sprouts
- 1 lime, cut into 6–8 wedges
- 1 medium carrot, peeled and thinly cut on the diagonal
- 1 recipe Spicy Thai Dressing (Page 33)
- 1 small red bell pepper, cored, seeded, and slice into fine strips
- 1 teaspoon sesame oil
- 1 teaspoon soy sauce

- 10 basil leaves, shredded (if possible Thai or lemon)

- 2 teaspoons vegetable oil

- 4 green onions, thinly cut

- 8 ounces dried rice noodles, cooked firm to the bite and washed under cold water

DIRECTIONS:

1. In a big container, toss the noodles with the oils and the soy sauce.

2. Blanch the snow peas in boiling water for half a minute and then wash them under cold water.

3. Put in the snow peas, bell pepper, and the carrot to the noodles and toss.

4. Sprinkle the Spicy Thai Dressing (Page 33) over the noodle mixture to taste, put in the basil, half of the green onions, and half of the bean sprouts, and toss thoroughly.

5. To serve, put the noodle salad on a chilled serving platter. Spread the rest of the green onions, remaining bean sprouts, and the peanuts over the top. Squeeze the juice of 2 lime wedges over the whole dish, and use the rest of the wedges as decorate. Serve instantly.

CRUNCHY COCONUT-FLAVORED SALAD

Yield: Servings 2–3

INGREDIENTS:

- 1 cup julienned jicama

- 1 medium cucumber, peeled, seeded, and julienned

- 1 recipe Coconut Marinade (Page 12)

- 2–3 tablespoons chopped fresh basil

DIRECTIONS:

1. Put the jicama, cucumber, and basil in a big container.

2. Pour the marinade over the vegetables and allow to rest in your fridge for minimum 2 hours before you serve.

CUCUMBER SALAD WITH LEMONGRASS

Yield: Servings 6–8

INGREDIENTS:

- ¼ cup minced mint
- ¼ cup minced parsley
- ½ cup shredded carrot
- ½ cup white vinegar
- 1 cup bean sprouts
- 1 cup cubed tart apple (such as Granny Smith)
- 1 garlic clove, very thoroughly minced
- 1 tablespoon fish sauce
- 1 tablespoon vegetable oil
- 1 Thai chili, very thoroughly minced
- 2 stalks lemongrass
- 3 cups thinly cut cucumber

DIRECTIONS:

1. In a small deep cooking pan, mix the vinegar, chili, and garlic. Bring the mixture to its boiling point. Cover the pan, take it off the heat, and allow to cool.

2. Trim and finely cut 1 lemongrass stalk. Put it in a small deep cooking pan with ½ cup of water, cover, and bring to its boiling point. Turn off heat and allow to cool.

3. Trim the rest of the lemongrass stalk, peel off the tough outer layers, and finely mince the white portion of the soft stalk within. Reserve roughly 1 tablespoon.

4. Mix the cucumber, bean sprouts, apple, carrot, mint, and parsley in a big mixing container. In a small container mix the fish sauce, oil, minced lemongrass, the vinegar mixture, and the lemongrass water.

5. Toss the vegetables with the lemongrass vinaigrette to taste.

FIERY BEEF SALAD

Yield: Servings 2–4

INGREDIENTS:

For the dressing:

- ¼ cup basil leaves
- ¼ cup lemon juice

- ¼ teaspoon black pepper

- 2 cloves garlic

- 2 tablespoons brown sugar

- 2 tablespoons chopped serrano chilies

- 2 tablespoons fish sauce

For the salad:

- ½ cup mint leaves

- 1 pound beef steak

- 1 small cucumber, finely cut

- 1 small red onion, finely cut

- 1 stalk lemongrass, outer leaves removed and discarded, inner stalk finely cut

- 1 tomato, finely cut

- Bibb or romaine lettuce leaves

- Salt and pepper to taste

DIRECTIONS:

1. Mix all of the dressing ingredients in a blender and pulse until well blended; set aside.

2. Flavour the steak with salt and pepper. Over a hot fire, grill to moderate-rare (or to your preference). Move the steak to a platter, cover using foil, and allow to rest for five to ten minutes before carving.

3. Cut the beef across the grain into thin slices.

4. Put the beef slices, any juices from the platter, and the rest of the salad ingredients, apart from the lettuce, in a big mixing container. Put in the dressing and toss to coat.

5. To serve, place lettuce leaves on separate plates and mound the beef mixture on top of the lettuce.

GRILLED CALAMARI SALAD

Yield: Servings 2–4

INGREDIENTS:

For the dressing:

- 1 small onion, thinly cut

- 1 stalk lemongrass, inner core finely chopped

- 1 tablespoon fish sauce

- 1–5 red chili peppers, seeded and chopped

- 3 kaffir lime leaves, chopped or 1 tablespoon lime zest

- 5 teaspoons lime juice

- 1 cup water

For the salad:

- 1 green onion, thinly cut

- 1 pound calamari, cleaned

- 6–8 sprigs cilantro, chopped

- Baby greens (not necessary)

- fifteen–20 mint leaves, chopped

DIRECTIONS:

1. Mix all the dressing ingredients in a small container; set aside.

2. Prepare a grill or broiler. Put the calamari on a broiler pan or in a grill basket and cook using high heat until soft, approximately 3 minutes per side. Allow to cool to room temperature.

3. Put the grilled calamari in a mixing container. Mix the dressing and pour it over the calamari.

4. If serving instantly, put in the mint, cilantro, and green onions. If you don't like this method, allow the calamari to marinate for maximum 1 hour before you serve, and then put in the additional ingredients.

5. To serve: Use individual cups or bowls to help capture some of the wonderful dressing. If you don't like this method, mound the calamari mixture over a bed of baby greens and spoon additional dressing over the top.

PAPAYA SALAD

Yield: Servings 4–6

INGREDIENTS:

- ½ cup long beans (green beans), cut into 1–inch pieces

- ½–1 teaspoon salt

- 1 medium papaya, peeled and julienned, or cut into little pieces

- 2 teaspoons fish sauce

- 2 tomatoes, thinly cut

- 3 jalapeño peppers, seeded and thinly cut

- 4 tablespoons Tamarind Concentrate (Page 20)

- 4–6 cloves of garlic, chopped crudely

- Sticky rice, cooked in accordance with package directions

DIRECTIONS:

1. Put the papaya on a sheet pan and drizzle it with salt. Allow the papaya stand for half an hour Pour off any juice and then squeeze the fruit with your hands to extract as much fluid as you can. Put the pulp of the papaya in a big food processor.

2. Put in the chilies and pulse for a short period of time to blend. Put in the rest of the ingredients except the tomato and pulse again until combined.

3. Move the papaya mixture to a serving container and decorate with tomato slices. Serve with sticky rice.

SHRIMP AND NOODLE SALAD

INGREDIENTS:

- ½–1 teaspoon dried red pepper flakes

- ¾ cup lime juice (roughly 4–5 limes)

- 1 clove garlic, minced

- 1 cup citrus fruit (oranges, grapefruit, tangerines, etc.) peeled, sectioned, and chopped

- 1 medium tomato, peeled, seeded, and chopped

- 1 stalk lemongrass, thoroughly minced (inner core only)

- 1 tablespoon brown sugar

- 1 tablespoon vegetable oil

- 2 tablespoons fish sauce

- 24 medium shrimp, peeled and deveined

- 3 green onions, cut

- 8 ounces rice noodles

- 1 cup chopped cilantro, plus extra for decoration

- 1 cup chopped mint leaves

- 1 cup chopped peanuts, plus extra for decoration
- Salt and ground pepper to taste

DIRECTIONS:

1. Soak the rice noodles in hot water for ten to twenty minutes or until tender. While the noodles are soaking, bring a big pot of water to boil.

2. In the meantime, in a big container, combine the lemongrass, citrus, peanuts, tomato, scallions, mint, and cilantro.

3. In a small container, mix the red pepper flakes, garlic, sugar, lime juice, and fish sauce. (Adjust seasoning to your taste.)

4. Drain the noodles from their soaking liquid and put in them to the boiling water. When the water returns to its boiling point, drain them again and wash meticulously with cold water. Allow the noodles to drain well.

5. Put in the noodles and the dressing to the citrus mixture and toss to blend. Set aside.

6. Brush the shrimp with the vegetable oil and sprinkle with salt and pepper. Grill or sauté for roughly two minutes per side or until done to your preference.

7. To serve, mound the noodles in the middle of a serving platter. Put the grilled shrimp on top and decorate with peanuts and cilantro.

Yield: Servings 6

SPICY RICE SALAD

Yield: Approximately 8 cups

INGREDIENTS:

For the dressing:
- ¼ cup hot chili oil
- ¼ cup lime juice
- ¼ cup sesame oil
- ½ cup fish sauce
- ½ cup rice vinegar

For the salad:

- 2 cups long-grained rice (if possible Jasmine)
- 2 carrots, peeled and diced
- 1 sweet red pepper, seeded and diced
- 1 serrano chili pepper, seeded and minced
- ¼–½ cup chopped mint
- ¼–½ cup chopped cilantro
- 1 pound cooked shrimp
- 1 cup chopped unsalted peanuts
- Lime wedges
- 4–6 green onions, trimmed and thinly cut

DIRECTIONS:

1. Whisk together all of the dressing ingredients; set aside.
2. Cook the rice in accordance with the package directions. Fluff the rice, then move it to a big mixing container. Allow the rice to cool slightly.
3. Pour roughly of the dressing over the rice and fluff to coat. Continue to fluff the rice every so frequently until it is completely cooled.
4. Put in the green onions, carrots, red pepper, serrano chili pepper, mint, cilantro, and shrimp to the rice. Toss with the rest of the dressing to taste.
5. To serve, place on separate plates and decorate with peanuts and lime wedges.

SPICY SHRIMP SALAD

Yield: Servings 2–4

INGREDIENTS:

For the dressing:
- 2 tablespoons prepared chili sauce
- 3 tablespoons sugar
- 4 tablespoons fish sauce
- 1 cup lime juice

For the salad:

- ¼ cup chopped mint

- ¾ pound cooked shrimp

- 1 small red onion, thinly cut

- 2 cucumbers, peeled and thinly cut

- 2 green onions, trimmed and thinly cut

- Bibb lettuce leaves

DIRECTIONS:

1. In a small container, mix all the dressing ingredients. Stir until the sugar dissolves completely.

2. In a big container, mix all of the salad ingredients apart from the lettuce. Pour the dressing over and toss to coat.

3. To serve, put the lettuce leaves on separate plates. Mound a portion of the shrimp salad on top of the leaves. Serve instantly.

SWEET-AND-SOUR CUCUMBER SALAD

INGREDIENTS:

- ½ cup rice or white vinegar

- 1 cup boiling water

- 1 small red onion, cut

- 1 teaspoon salt

- 2 medium cucumbers, seeded and cut

- 2 Thai chilies, seeded and minced

- 5 tablespoons sugar

DIRECTIONS:

1. In a small container, mix the sugar, salt, and boiling water. Stir to meticulously dissolve sugar and salt. Put in the vinegar and allow the vinaigrette to cool completely.

2. Put the cucumbers, onion slices, and the chili peppers in a medium-sized container. Pour the dressing over the vegetables. Cover and let marinate in your fridge minimum until cold, if possible overnight.

Yield: Servings 2–4

THAI DINNER SALAD

Yield: Servings 2–4

INGREDIENTS:

For the dressing:

- ¾ teaspoon rice wine vinegar
- 1 clove garlic, minced
- 1 tablespoon lemon juice
- 1 tablespoon water
- 2 tablespoons fish sauce
- 2 teaspoons sugar
- Pinch of red pepper flakes

For the salad:

- ¼ cup chopped cilantro
- ¼ cup chopped mint leaves
- 1 cucumber, peeled, seeded, and diced
- 1 small head of romaine or Bibb lettuce, torn into bitesized pieces
- 2 small carrots, grated
- Chopped unsalted peanuts (not necessary)

DIRECTIONS:

1. In a small container, mix together all of the salad dressing ingredients; set aside.
2. In a big container, toss together all of the salad ingredients. Put in dressing to taste and toss until thoroughly coated. Drizzle chopped peanuts over the top of each salad, if you wish.

THAILAND BAMBOO SHOOTS

Yield: Servings 4

INGREDIENTS:

- 1 20-ounce can of bamboo shoots, shredded, liquid reserved

- 1 teaspoon fish sauce
- 1 teaspoon ground dried chili pepper
- 2 green onions, cut
- 2 tablespoons finely crushed peanuts, divided
- Juice of ½ lime
- Sticky rice, cooked in accordance with package directions

DIRECTIONS:

1. Put the shredded bamboo shoots and roughly ¼ cup (half) of the reserved bamboo liquid in a moderate-sized deep cooking pan. Bring the contents of the pan to its boiling point, reduce heat, and allow to simmer until soft, approximately five minutes. Turn off the heat.
2. Mix in the lime juice, chili pepper, green onions, fish sauce, and 1 tablespoon of the peanuts.
3. Serve with sticky rice, sprinkled with the rest of the peanuts.

THAILAND SEAFOOD SALAD

Yield: Servings 4–6

INGREDIENTS:

- ¼ cup fish sauce
- ½ pound salad shrimp
- ½ pound squid rings, poached in salted water for half a minute
- 1 (6-ounce) can chopped clams, drained
- 1 clove garlic, minced
- 1 green onion, trimmed and thinly cut
- 1 small onion, finely chopped
- 1 small serrano chili, seeded and finely chopped
- 1 stalk celery, cleaned and thinly cut
- 1 stalk lemongrass, outer leaves removed, inner core minced
- 2 medium cucumbers, peeled, halved, seeded, and super slimly cut
- 2 tablespoons chopped mint
- Bibb lettuce leaves

- Sugar to taste

DIRECTIONS:

1. In a big mixing container, gently mix the squid, shrimp, clams, cucumber, and celery; set aside.

2. In a small mixing container, mix together the onion, lemongrass, serrano chili, mint, garlic, green onion, and fish sauce. Put in sugar to taste.

3. Pour the dressing over the seafood mixture, tossing to coat. Cover and allow it to sit for minimum 30 minutes before you serve.

4. To serve, place lettuce leaves in the middle of four to 6 plates. Mound the seafood salad on top of the lettuce leaves.

ZESTY MELON SALAD

Yield: Servings 4–6

INGREDIENTS:

- ¼ cup honey
- ¼ teaspoon salt
- 1 serrano chili, seeded and minced (for a hotter salad, leave the seeds in)
- 2 cucumbers, peeled, halved, seeded, and cut
- 6 cups assorted melon cubes
- 6–8 tablespoons lime juice
- Zest of 1 lime

DIRECTIONS:

1. In a big mixing container, mix the melon and the cucumber.

2. Combine the rest of the ingredients together in a small container. Pour over the fruit and toss thoroughly to coat.

3. Serve instantly, or if you prefer a zestier flavor, let the salad sit for maximum 2 hours to allow the chili flavor to develop.

GREEN CURRY BEEF

Yield: Servings 4–6

INGREDIENTS:

- ¼ cup (or to taste) Green Curry Paste
- ¼ cup brown sugar
- ¼ cup fish sauce
- 1 cup basil
- 1 pound eggplant (Japanese, Thai, or a combination), cut into ¼-inch slices
- 1½ pounds sirloin, cut into fine strips
- 2 cans coconut milk, thick cream separated from the milk
- 6 serrano chilies, stemmed, seeded, and cut in half along the length

DIRECTIONS:

1. Put the thick cream from the coconut milk and the curry paste in a big soup pot and stir until blended. Put on moderate to high heat and bring to its boiling point. Decrease the heat and simmer for two to three minutes.
2. Put in the beef and the coconut milk, stirring to blend. Return the mixture to a simmer.
3. Put in the sugar and the fish sauce, stirring until the sugar dissolves, approximately 2 minutes.
4. Put in the eggplant and simmer for one to two minutes.
5. Put in the serrano chilies and cook one minute more.
6. Turn off the heat and mix in the basil.

CURRIED BEEF AND POTATO STEW

Yield: Servings 4

INGREDIENTS:

- ¼ cup Tamarind Concentrate (Page 20)
- ½ cup brown sugar
- ½ cup unsalted roasted peanuts, chopped
- ½–¾ cup prepared Massaman Curry Paste (Page 19)
- 1 big onion, chopped
- 1 big russet potato, peeled and slice into bite-sized cubes
- 1 cup chopped fresh pineapple
- 1½ pounds beef stew meat, cut into bite-sized cubes

- 2 (14-ounce) cans coconut milk

- 2–3 tablespoons vegetable oil

- 7 tablespoons fish sauce

- Jasmine rice, cooked in accordance with package directions

DIRECTIONS:

1. Heat the oil in a big soup pot on moderate to high heat. Once the oil is hot, brown the meat on all sides. Put in the onion and cook until translucent, approximately two to three minutes.

2. Put in enough water to just cover the meat and onions. Bring to its boiling point, reduce heat, cover, and simmer for thirty to 60 minutes.

3. Put in the potatoes and carry on simmering for fifteen more minutes. (The potatoes will not be fairly thoroughly cooked now.)

4. Strain the solids from the broth, saving for later both.

5. In another soup pot, mix the coconut milk with the curry paste until well mixed. Bring the contents to a simmer on moderate to high heat and cook for two to three minutes.

6. Put in the reserved meat and potato mixture, the sugar, fish sauce, and tamarind, stirring until the sugar dissolves. Put in some of the reserved broth to thin the sauce to desired consistency.

7. Mix in the pineapple and carry on simmering until the potatoes are thoroughly cooked.

8. To serve, place some Jasmine rice in the center of individual serving plates and spoon the stew over the top. Decorate using the chopped peanuts.

RED BEEF CURRY

Yield: Servings 4

INGREDIENTS:

- ¼ cup chopped basil

- ½ cup plus 2 tablespoons coconut milk

- 1 green or red sweet pepper, seeded and cubed

- 1 pound lean beef, cut into fine strips

- 1 tablespoon vegetable oil

- 1–3 tablespoons (to taste) fish sauce

- 2 tablespoons (roughly) ground peanuts

- 2 tablespoons Red Curry Paste (Page 17)
- Rice, cooked in accordance with package directions
- Sugar to taste

DIRECTIONS:

1. Heat the oil in a big sauté pan using low heat. Put in the curry paste and cook, stirring continuously, until aromatic, approximately one minute.
2. Mix in the ½ cup of coconut milk and bring the mixture to a simmer. Put in the beef strips and poach for five minutes.
3. Put in the peanuts and continue to poach for another five minutes.
4. Put in the fish sauce and sugar to taste; carry on cooking until the mixture is almost dry, then put in the sweet pepper and basil and cook for 5 more minutes.
5. Serve with rice.

HOT AND SOUR BEEF

Yield: Servings 1–2

NGREDIENTS:

- 1 green onion, trimmed and thinly cut
- 1 tablespoon dark, sweet soy sauce
- 1 tablespoon fish sauce
- 1 tablespoon lime juice
- 1 teaspoon chopped cilantro
- 1 teaspoon dried chili powder
- 1 teaspoon honey
- 1½ pound sirloin steak
- 3 tablespoons chopped onion
- Salt and pepper to taste

DIRECTIONS:

1. Make the sauce by meticulously combining the first 8 ingredients; set aside.

2. Flavour the steak with salt and pepper, then grill or broil it to your preferred doneness. Take away the steak from the grill, cover using foil, and allow to rest for five to ten minutes.

3. Thinly slice the steak, cutting across the grain.

4. Position the pieces on a serving platter or on 1 or 2 dinner plates. Ladle the sauce over the top. Serve with rice and a side vegetable.

GRILLED GINGER BEEF

Yield: Servings 6

INGREDIENTS:

- 1 (2-inch) piece of ginger, minced
- 1 (3-inch) piece ginger, cut in half
- 1 cinnamon stick
- 1 onion, cut in half
- 1 pound green vegetables
- 1 small package of rice noodles
- 2 dried red chili peppers
- 2 stalks lemongrass
- 2 tablespoons (or to taste) soy sauce
- 5 cloves garlic
- 6 (6-ounce) strip steaks
- 6 scallions, minced
- 8 cups low-salt beef broth
- Salt and pepper to taste

DIRECTIONS:

1. Put the beef broth, lemongrass, and garlic in a big pot; bring to its boiling point.

2. Meanwhile, put the ginger and onion halves, cut-side down, in a dry frying pan using high heat and cook until black. Put in the onion and ginger to the broth mixture.

3. Put the cinnamon and dried chili peppers in the dry frying pan and toast on moderate heat for a minute; put in to the broth mixture.

4. Lower the heat and simmer the broth for a couple of hours. Cool, strain, and place in your fridge overnight.

5. Before you are ready to eat, remove the broth from the fridge and skim off any fat that may have collected. Bring the broth to a simmer and put in the minced ginger.

6. Soak the rice noodles in hot water for ten to twenty minutes or until soft; drain.

7. Blanch the vegetables for approximately one minute. Using a slotted spoon, remove them from the boiling water and shock them in cold water.

8. Flavour the broth to taste with the soy sauce. Flavour the steaks with salt and pepper and grill or broil to your preference.

9. To serve, slice the steaks into fine strips (cutting across the grain) and put them in 6 big bowls. Put in a portion of noodles and vegetables to the bowls and ladle the broth over the top.

THAI BEEF WITH RICE NOODLES

Yield: Servings 4–6

INGREDIENTS:

- ¼ cup soy sauce
- ½ pound dried rice noodles
- ¾ pound sirloin, trimmed of all fat, washed and patted dry
- 1 pound greens (such as spinach or bok choy), cleaned and slice into ½-inch strips
- 2 eggs, beaten
- 2 tablespoons dark brown sugar
- 2 tablespoons fish sauce
- 2 tablespoons minced garlic
- 5 tablespoons vegetable oil, divided
- Crushed dried red pepper flakes to taste
- Freshly ground black pepper
- Rice vinegar to taste

DIRECTIONS:

1. Cut the meat into two-inch-long, ½–inch-wide strips.
2. Cover the noodles with warm water for five minutes, then drain.

3. In a small container, mix the soy sauce, fish sauce, brown sugar, and black pepper; set aside.

4. Heat a wok or heavy frying pan using high heat. Put in roughly 2 tablespoons of the vegetable oil. Once the oil is hot, but not smoking, put in the garlic. After stirring for 5 seconds, put in the greens and stir-fry for roughly two minutes; set aside.

5. Put in 2 more tablespoons of oil to the wok. Put in the beef and stir-fry until browned on all sides, approximately 2 minutes; set aside.

6. Heat 1 tablespoon of oil in the wok and put in the noodles. Toss until warmed through, roughly two minutes; set aside.

7. Heat the oil remaining in the wok. Put in the eggs and cook, without stirring until they are set, approximately half a minute. Break up the eggs slightly and mix in the reserved noodles, beef, and greens, and the red pepper flakes. Mix the reserved soy mixture, then put in it to the wok. Toss to coat and heat through. Serve instantly with rice vinegar to drizzle over the top.

MINTY STIR-FRIED BEEF

Yield: Servings 4–6

INGREDIENTS:

- ¼ cup chopped garlic
- ¼ cup chopped yellow or white onion
- ¼ cup vegetable oil
- ½ cup chopped mint leaves
- ½–¾ cup water
- 1 pound flank steak, cut across the grain into fine strips
- 1 tablespoon sugar
- 3 tablespoons fish sauce
- 7–14 (to taste) serrano chilies, seeded and crudely chopped

DIRECTIONS:

1. Using a mortar and pestle or a food processor, grind together the chilies, garlic, and onion.

2. Heat the oil on moderate to high heat in a wok or big frying pan. Put in the ground chili mixture to the oil and stir-fry for one to two minutes.

3. Put in the beef and stir-fry until it just starts to brown.

4. Put in the rest of the ingredients, adjusting the amount of water depending on how thick you desire the sauce.

5. Serve with sufficient Jasmine rice.

CHILIED BEEF

Yield: Servings 2–4

INGREDIENTS:

- ¼ cup white vinegar
- 1 big red onion, cut
- 1 pound flank steak
- 1 teaspoon dried red pepper flakes
- 2 tablespoons fish sauce
- 3 serrano chilies, stems removed and cut
- 4 scallions, trimmed and thinly cut
- Bibb or romaine lettuce leaves
- Juice of 1 big lime

DIRECTIONS:

1. Put the cut chilies in a small container with the vinegar; allow it to stand for minimum fifteen minutes.
2. Grill or broil the flank steak to your desired doneness. Remove from the grill, cover using foil, and allow it to stand ten minutes. Thinly slice the streak across the grain.
3. Put the beef slices in a big container. Put in the red onion, scallions, lime juice, and red pepper flakes; toss all of the ingredients together. Cover the dish, place in your fridge, and let marinate for minimum 1 hour.
4. Before you serve, let the beef return to room temperature. Mound the beef on top of lettuce leaves and serve with white rice. Pass the serrano/vinegar sauce separately.

PORK AND EGGPLANT STIR-FRY

INGREDIENTS:

- 3 tablespoons vegetable oil

- ½ pound ground pork
- ½ teaspoon freshly ground pepper
- 1 tablespoon fish sauce
- 1 tablespoon Yellow Bean Sauce (Page 24)
- 1 pound Japanese eggplant, cut into ¼-inch slices
- ¼ cup chicken stock
- 2 tablespoons (or to taste) sugar
- 5–10 cloves garlic, mashed

DIRECTIONS:

1. Heat the oil in a wok or big frying pan on moderate to high heat. Once the oil is hot, put in the garlic and stir-fry until aromatic, approximately half a minute.
2. Put in the pork and continue to stir-fry until the pork loses its color, approximately one minute.
3. Put in the pepper, fish sauce, bean sauce, and eggplant; cook for a minute.
4. Put in the chicken stock. Continue to stir-fry for a couple of minutes.
5. Mix in the sugar to taste and cook until the eggplant is thoroughly cooked, approximately 2 more minutes.

PORK WITH GARLIC AND CRUSHED BLACK PEPPER

Yield: Servings 2

INGREDIENTS:

- 4 tablespoons vegetable oil
- 1 pork tenderloin, trimmed of all fat and slice into medallions about ¼-inch thick
- ¼ cup sweet black soy sauce
- 2 tablespoons brown sugar
- 2 tablespoons fish sauce
- 2–2½ teaspoons black peppercorns, crudely ground
- 10–20 garlic cloves, mashed

DIRECTIONS:

1. Put the garlic and the black pepper in a small food processor and process for a short period of time to make a crude paste; set aside.

2. Heat the oil in a wok or big frying pan on moderate to high heat. Once the oil is hot, put in the garlic-pepper paste and stir-fry until the garlic turns gold.

3. Increase the heat to high and put in the pork medallions; stir-fry for half a minute.

4. Put in the soy sauce and brown sugar, stirring until the sugar is dissolved.

5. Put in the fish sauce and carry on cooking until the pork is thoroughly cooked, approximately another one to two minutes.

BANGKOK-STYLE ROASTED PORK TENDERLOIN

Yield: Servings 4

INGREDIENTS:

- ¼ teaspoon ground cardamom
- ¼ teaspoon ground ginger
- ¼–½ teaspoon freshly ground black pepper
- ½ cup chicken, pork, or vegetable stock, or water
- 1 teaspoon salt
- 2 (1-pound) pork tenderloins, trimmed
- Olive oil

DIRECTIONS:

1. Put rack on bottom third of the oven, then preheat your oven to 500 degrees.
2. Mix the spices in a small container.
3. Rub each of the tenderloins with half of the spice mixture and a small amount of olive oil. Put the tenderloins in a roasting pan and cook for about ten minutes.
4. Turn the tenderloins over and roast for ten more minutes or until done to your preference.
5. Move the pork to a serving platter, cover using foil, and allow to rest.

6. Pour off any fat that has collected in the roasting pan. Put the pan on the stovetop using high heat and put in the stock (or water). Bring to its boiling point, scraping the bottom of the pan to loosen any cookedon bits. Sprinkle with salt and pepper to taste.

7. To serve, slice the tenderloins into thin slices. Pour a small amount of the sauce on top, passing more separately at the table.

CHIANG MAI BEEF

Yield: Servings 4–6

INGREDIENTS:

- 1 pound lean ground beef
- 1 tablespoon chopped garlic
- 1 tablespoon small dried chilies
- 1 tablespoon vegetable oil
- 2 cups uncooked long-grained rice
- 2 green onions, trimmed and cut
- 3¼ cups water
- 3–4 tablespoons soy sauce
- Fish sauce

DIRECTIONS:

1. In a big deep cooking pan, bring the water to its boiling point, then mix in the rice. Cover, decrease the heat to low, and cook until the water is absorbed, approximately twenty minutes.

2. Place the cooked rice in a big mixing container and let cool completely.

3. Put in the ground beef and soy sauce to the rice, mixing meticulously. (I find using my hands works best.)

4. Split the rice-beef mixture into 8 to 12 equivalent portions, depending on the size you prefer, and form them into loose balls. Cover each ball in foil, ensuring to secure them well.

5. Steam the rice balls for twenty-five to thirty minutes or until thoroughly cooked.

6. While the rice is steaming, heat the vegetable oil in a small frying pan. Put in the garlic and the dried chilies and sauté until the garlic is golden. Move the garlic and the chilies to a paper towel to drain.

7. To serve, remove the rice packets from the foil, slightly smash them, and put on serving plates. Pass the garlic-chili mixture, the green onions, and the fish sauce separately to be used as condiments at the table.

BARBECUED PORK ON RICE

Yield: Servings 2–3

INGREDIENTS:

- 1 cucumber, thinly cut
- 1 green onion, trimmed and thinly cut
- 1 hard-boiled egg, peeled
- 1 pork tenderloin, trimmed of surplus fat
- 1 tablespoon sesame seeds, toasted
- 1 teaspoon Chinese 5-spice powder
- 1½ cups water
- 2 tablespoons flour
- 2 tablespoons rice vinegar
- 2 tablespoons soy sauce
- 2 tablespoons sugar
- Jasmine rice, cooked in accordance with package directions

DIRECTIONS:

1. Cut the tenderloin into medallions roughly ¼-inch thick. Put the medallions in a mixing container.
2. Mix the sugar, soy sauce, and 5-spice powder in a small container.
3. Pour the soy mixture over pork strips and toss the strips until meticulously coated. Let marinate minimum 30 minutes, but if possible overnight.
4. Preheat your oven to 350 degrees. Put the pork pieces in a single layer on a baking sheet lined using foil. Reserve any remaining marinade.
5. Bake the pork for roughly 1 hour. The pork with be firm and rather dry, but not burned. It will also have a reddish color.

6. Put the reserved marinade in a small deep cooking pan and heat to boiling. Remove the heat and put in the peeled egg, rolling it in the sauce to color it. Take away the egg and set it aside. When sufficiently cool to handle, cut it into thin pieces.

7. Mix the flour and water, and put in it to the marinade. Bring to its boiling point to thicken, then turn off the heat.

8. Put in the vinegar and the sesame seeds. Adjust seasoning by putting in additional sugar and/or soy sauce.

9. To serve, place some Jasmine rice in the middle of each plate. Fan a few pieces of the pork around 1 side of the rice. Fan some cucumber slices and cut hard-boiled egg around the other side. Ladle some of the sauce over the pork and drizzle with the green onion slices.

LEMONGRASS PORK

Yield: Servings 2

INGREDIENTS:

- ¼ cup chopped shallots
- ¼ cup coconut milk
- ¼ cup minced garlic
- ¼ cup whiskey
- ½ cup brown sugar
- ½ cup chopped lemongrass stalks (inner white portion only)
- ½ cup dark soy sauce
- ½ cup fish sauce
- 1 pound lean pork, cut into bite-sized pieces
- 1 teaspoon cayenne pepper
- 3 tablespoons sesame oil

DIRECTIONS:

1. In a moderate-sized-sized deep cooking pan, mix the brown sugar, fish sauce, soy sauce, lemongrass, whiskey, shallots, and garlic. Over moderate heat, bring to its boiling point and cook until the mixture is reduced to half. Take away the marinade from the heat and let it cool to room temperature. Mix in the coconut milk, sesame oil, and cayenne pepper.

2. Put the pork and the marinade in a big Ziplock bag. Marinate the pork in your fridge for minimum three hours, or overnight.

3. Drain the meat, saving for later the marinade. Thread the meat onto metal skewers (or soaked bamboo skewers), and grill or broil to your preference.

4. Put the reserved marinade in a small deep cooking pan and bring it to its boiling point on moderate to high heat. Lower the heat and simmer the marinade for two to three minutes. Use the marinade as a dipping sauce for the pork.

PORK AND SPINACH CURRY

Yield: Servings 1–2

INGREDIENTS:

- ½ cup lean pork strips
- ½ lime
- ½ pound baby spinach
- 1 cup coconut milk, divided
- 1 tablespoon Red Curry Paste (Page 17)
- 2 cups water
- 2 tablespoons sugar
- 3–4 kaffir lime leaves, crumbled
- 4 tablespoons fish sauce
- Rice, cooked in accordance with package directions

DIRECTIONS:

1. In a moderate-sized-sized deep cooking pan, heat ½ cup of the coconut milk and the curry paste on moderate to low heat, stirring to blend meticulously. Cook for five minutes, stirring continuously, so that the sauce does not burn.

2. Put in the pork cubes, the rest of the coconut milk, and the water. Return the mixture to a simmer and allow to cook for five minutes. Squeeze the juice of the lime half into the curry. Put in the lime half.

3. Mix in the kaffir lime leaves, fish sauce, and sugar. Continue simmering for five to 10 more minutes or until the pork is thoroughly cooked. Take away the lime half.

4. Put in the baby spinach and cook for a minute.

5. Serve over rice.

THAI-STYLE BEEF WITH BROCCOLI

Yield: Servings 2–4

INGREDIENTS:

- ½ of a 7–8-ounce package of rice sticks
- 1 cup broccoli pieces
- 1 medium shallot, chopped
- 1 pound lean beef, cut into bite-sized pieces
- 1 tablespoon preserved soy beans (not necessary)
- 1 teaspoon chili powder
- 2 cups water
- 2 tablespoons brown sugar
- 2 tablespoons fish sauce
- 2 tablespoons sweet soy sauce
- 3 tablespoons vegetable oil
- Hot sauce (not necessary)
- Lime wedges (not necessary)

DIRECTIONS:

1. Heat the vegetable oil in a wok on moderate to high heat. Put in the shallot and stir-fry until it starts to become tender. Put in the chili powder and continue to stir-fry until well blended.

2. Put in the brown sugar, fish sauce, soy sauce, and soy beans; stir-fry for half a minute.

3. Put in the beef and continue to stir-fry until the beef is almost done, roughly two minutes.

4. Mix in the water and bring it to its boiling point. Put in the rice sticks, stirring until they start to cook. Lower the heat to moderate, cover, and allow to cook for half a minute. Stir and decrease the heat to moderate-low, cover, and allow to cook for about three minutes.

5. Put in the broccoli pieces, cover, and cook for a minute. Take away the wok from the heat and tweak seasoning to taste.

6. Serve with wedges of lime and hot sauce passed separately at the table.

PORK WITH TOMATOES AND STICKY RICE

Yield: Servings 2

INGREDIENTS:

- ½ pound crudely chopped lean pork
- ½ teaspoon salt
- ½ teaspoon shrimp paste
- 1 tablespoon chopped garlic
- 1 tablespoon fish sauce
- 1 tablespoon vegetable oil
- 1 teaspoon brown sugar
- 2 tablespoons chopped shallot
- 20 cherry tomatoes, quartered
- 7 small dried chilies
- Sticky rice, cooked in accordance with package directions

DIRECTIONS:

1. Trim the chilies of their stems and shake out the seeds. Cut them into little pieces, cover them with warm water, and allow them to soak for about twenty minutes to tenderize; drain.
2. Using a food processor or mortar and pestle, grind (or process) the chilies and salt together until a thick paste is formed. Put in the shrimp paste, shallot, and garlic. Process until well blended; set aside.
3. Heat a wok or heavy-bottomed frying pan using low heat. Put in the vegetable oil and heat for a minute. Put in the chili purée and cook for roughly three minutes or until the color of the paste deepens.
4. Raise the heat to moderate and put in the pork; stir-fry for a minute. Put in the tomatoes and carry on cooking for three to four minutes, stirring regularly.
5. Mix in the fish sauce and brown sugar; simmer for a couple of minutes. Adjust seasoning to taste.
6. Serve this beef dish with sticky rice either warm or at room temperature.

CINNAMON STEWED BEEF

Yield: Servings 4

INGREDIENTS:

- 1 (2-inch) piece of cinnamon stick
- 1 bay leaf
- 1 celery stalk, cut
- 1 clove garlic, smashed
- 1 pound beef sirloin, trimmed of all fat and slice into 1-inch cubes
- 1½ quarts water
- 2 tablespoons sugar
- 2 tablespoons sweet soy sauce
- 2 whole star anise
- 5 sprigs cilantro
- 5 tablespoons soy sauce

DIRECTIONS:

1. Put the water in a big soup pot and bring to its boiling point. Decrease the heat to low and put in the rest of the ingredients.

2. Simmer, putting in more water if required, for minimum 2 hours or until the beef is completely soft. If possible, let the stewed beef sit in your fridge overnight.

3. To serve, place noodles or rice on the bottom of 4 soup bowls. Put in pieces of beef and then ladle broth over. Drizzle with chopped cilantro or cut green onions if you prefer. Pass a vinegar-chili sauce of your choice as a dip for the beef.

BASIL CHICKEN

Yield: Servings 4–6

INGREDIENTS:

- 1 big onion, cut into thin slices
- 1 tablespoon water
- 1½ cups chopped basil leaves, divided
- 1½ tablespoons soy sauce

- 1½ teaspoons sugar

- 2 tablespoons fish sauce

- 2 tablespoons vegetable oil

- 2 whole boneless, skinless chicken breasts, cut into 1-inch cubes

- 3 cloves garlic, minced

- 3 Thai chilies, seeded and thinly cut

DIRECTIONS:

1. In a moderate-sized-sized container, mix the fish sauce, the soy sauce, water, and sugar. Put in the chicken cubes and stir to coat. Let marinate for about ten minutes.

2. In a big frying pan or wok, heat oil on moderate to high heat. Put in the onion and stir-fry for two to three minutes. Put in the chilies and garlic and carry on cooking for another half a minute.

3. Using a slotted spoon, remove the chicken from the marinade and put in it to the frying pan (reserve the marinade.) Stir-fry until almost thoroughly cooked, approximately 3 minutes.

4. Put in the reserved marinade and cook for another half a minute. Take away the frying pan from the heat and mix in 1 cup of the basil.

5. Decorate using the rest of the basil, and serve with rice.

BRANDIED CHICKEN

INGREDIENTS:

- ¼ cup vegetable oil

- 1 (1-inch) piece ginger, cut

- 1 teaspoon salt

- 1 whole roasting chicken, washed and trimmed of surplus fat

- 2 shots brandy

- 2 tablespoons black soy sauce

- 6 tablespoons soy sauce

- 8 cloves garlic, minced

DIRECTIONS:

1. Fill a pot big enough to hold the whole chicken roughly full of water. Bring the water to its boiling point using high heat. Lower the heat to moderate and cautiously put in the chicken to the pot. Regulate the heat so that the water is just simmering.

2. Poach the whole chicken for twenty minutes to half an hour or until thoroughly cooked. Cautiously remove the chicken from the pot, ensuring to drain the hot water from the cavity of the bird. Position the chicken aside to cool.

3. Take away the skin from the bird and discard. Take away the meat from the chicken and cut it into 1-inch pieces; set aside. (This portion of the recipe can be done 1 or 2 days in advance.)

4. Put in the oil to a big frying pan or wok and heat on medium. Put in the soy sauces, salt, and garlic. Stir-fry until the garlic starts to tenderize, approximately half a minute to one minute.

5. Put in the chicken pieces, stirring to coat. Mix in the brandy and the ginger.

6. Cover the frying pan or wok, decrease the heat to low, and simmer five to ten more minutes.

CHICKEN WITH BLACK PEPPER AND GARLIC

Yield: Servings 4–6

INGREDIENTS:

- 1 cup fish sauce
- 1 tablespoon whole black peppercorns
- 1 teaspoon sugar
- 2 pounds boneless, skinless chicken breasts, cut into strips
- 3 tablespoons vegetable oil
- 5 cloves garlic, cut in half

DIRECTIONS:

1. Using either a mortar and pestle or a food processor, mix the black peppercorns with the garlic.

2. Put the chicken strips in a big mixing container. Put in the garlic-pepper mixture and the fish sauce, and stir until blended.

3. Cover the container, place in your fridge, and let marinate for twenty minutes to half an hour.

4. Heat the vegetable oil on moderate heat in a wok or frying pan. When it is hot, put in the chicken mixture and stir-fry until thoroughly cooked, approximately 3 to five minutes.

5. Mix in the sugar. Put in additional sugar or fish sauce to taste.

CHILI-FRIED CHICKEN

INGREDIENTS:

- ½ teaspoon ground coriander
- ½ teaspoon white pepper
- 1½ teaspoons salt, divided
- 2 small onions, thinly cut
- 2 tablespoons vegetable oil
- 3 pounds chicken pieces, washed and patted dry
- 3 tablespoons Tamarind Concentrate (Page 20)
- 8 big red chilies, seeded and chopped
- Pinch of turmeric
- Vegetable oil for deep-frying

DIRECTIONS:

1. In a small container mix the tamarind, turmeric, coriander, 1 teaspoon of the salt, and the pepper.

2. Put the chicken pieces in a big Ziplock bag. Pour the tamarind mixture over the chicken, seal the bag, and marinate minimum 2 hours or overnight in your fridge.

3. In a small sauté pan, heat 2 tablespoons of vegetable oil on moderate heat. Put in the red chilies, onions, and the rest of the salt; sauté for five minutes. Set aside to cool slightly.

4. Move the chili mixture to a food processor and pulse for a short period of time to make a coarse sauce.

5. Drain the chicken and discard the marinade. Deep-fry the chicken pieces in hot oil until the skin is golden and the bones are crunchy. Take away the cooked chicken to paper towels to drain.

6. Put the cooked chicken in a big mixing container. Pour the chili sauce over the chicken and toss until each piece is uniformly coated.

Yield: Servings 4–6

FRAGRANT ROAST CHICKEN

Yield: Servings 2–4

INGREDIENTS:

For the marinade:

- ½ cup fish sauce
- ½ cup sweet dark soy sauce
- 1 tablespoon freshly ground black pepper
- 2 tablespoons crushed garlic
- 2 tablespoons freshly grated gingerroot

For the stuffing:

- ½ cup chopped cilantro
- ½ cup chopped mushrooms
- ½ cup cut bruised lemongrass stalks
- ½ cup fresh grated galangal
- ½ cup freshly grated ginger
- 1 roasting chicken, cleaned and patted dry

DIRECTIONS:

1. Mix all of the marinade ingredients in a plastic bag big enough to hold the whole chicken. Put in the chicken, ensuring to coat the whole bird with the marinade. Put the chicken in your fridge and leave overnight.
2. Take away the chicken from the plastic bag, saving for later the marinade.
3. Put all of the stuffing ingredients in a big mixing container. Mix in the reserved marinade.
4. Fill the bird's cavity and place it breast side up in a roasting pan. Put the roasting pan in a preheated 400 degree oven and roast for 50 to 60 minutes, or until the juices run clear.

GINGER CHICKEN

Yield: Servings 2

INGREDIENTS:

- 1 cup cut domestic mushrooms
- 1 tablespoon chopped garlic

- 1 whole boneless, skinless chicken breast, cut into bite-sized pieces

- 2 tablespoons dark soy sauce

- 2 tablespoons fish sauce

- 2 tablespoons oyster sauce

- 2–3 habanero or bird's eye chilis

- 3 green onions, trimmed and slice into 1-inch pieces

- 3 tablespoons chopped onion

- 3 tablespoons grated ginger

- 3 tablespoons vegetable oil

- Cilantro

- Jasmine rice, cooked in accordance with package directions

- Pinch of sugar

DIRECTIONS:

1. In a small container mix the fish, soy, and oyster sauces; set aside.

2. Heat the oil in a big wok until super hot. Put in the garlic and chicken, and stir-fry just until the chicken starts to change color.

3. Put in the reserved sauce and cook until it starts to simmer while stirring continuously.

4. Put in the mushrooms, ginger, sugar, onion, and chilies; simmer until the chicken is thoroughly cooked, approximately eight minutes.

5. To serve, ladle the chicken over Jasmine rice and top with green onion and cilantro.

JUNGLE CHICKEN

Yield: Servings 2–3

INGREDIENTS:

- ½ cup coconut milk

- 1 stalk lemongrass, inner portion roughly chopped

- 1 whole boneless, skinless chicken breast, cut into fine strips

- 10–fifteen basil leaves

- 2 (2-inch-long, ½-inch wide) strips of lime peel

- 2 tablespoons vegetable oil

- 2–4 serrano chilies, stems and seeds removed

- 2–4 tablespoons fish sauce

DIRECTIONS:

1. Put the chilies, lemongrass, and lime peel into a food processor and pulse until ground.

2. Heat the oil on moderate to high heat in a wok or big frying pan. Put in the chili mixture and sauté for one to two minutes.

3. Mix in the coconut milk and cook for a couple of minutes.

4. Put in the chicken and cook until the chicken is thoroughly cooked, approximately five minutes.

5. Decrease the heat to low and put in the fish sauce and basil leaves to taste.

6. Serve with sufficient Jasmine rice.

LEMONGRASS CHICKEN SKEWERS

INGREDIENTS:

- 12 big cubes chicken breast meat, a little over 1 ounce each

- 2 tablespoons vegetable oil, divided

- 2 teaspoons fish sauce

- 5 stalks lemongrass, trimmed

- Black pepper

- Juice of 1 lime

- Pinch of dried red pepper flakes

- Pinch of sugar

- Sea salt to taste

DIRECTIONS:

1. Remove 2 inches from the thick end of each stalk of lemongrass; set aside. Bruise 4 of the lemongrass stalks using the back of a knife. Take away the tough outer layer of the fifth stalk, exposing the soft core; mince.

2. Skewer 3 cubes of chicken on each lemongrass stalk. Drizzle the skewers with the minced lemongrass and black pepper, and sprinkle with 1 tablespoon of oil. Cover using plastic wrap and place in your fridge for twelve to one day.

3. Chop all of the reserved lemongrass stalk ends. Put in a small deep cooking pan and cover with water. Bring to its boiling point, cover, and let reduce until roughly 2 tablespoons of liquid is left; strain. Return the liquid to the deep cooking pan and further reduce to 1 tablespoon.

4. Mix the lemongrass liquid with the red pepper flakes, lime juice, fish sauce, sugar, and remaining tablespoon of oil; set aside.

5. Prepare a grill to high heat. Grill the chicken skewers for roughly two to three minutes per side, or until done to your preference.

6. To serve, spoon a little of the lemongrass sauce over the top of each skewer and drizzle with sea salt.

RED CHILI CHICKEN

Yield: Servings 2

INGREDIENTS:

- 1 tablespoon vegetable oil

- ½ cup coconut milk

- 1 whole boneless, skinless chicken breast, cut into bite-sized pieces

- 2 kaffir lime leaves or 2 (2-inch-long, ½–inch wide) pieces of lime zest

- 1 tablespoon basil leaves

- 2 tablespoons fish sauce

- 1 tablespoon brown sugar

- 4 ounces Thai eggplant (green peas can be substituted)

- 1–3 tablespoons Red Curry Paste (Page 17)

DIRECTIONS:

1. In a big frying pan or wok, heat the oil on moderate to high heat. Mix in the curry paste and cook until aromatic, approximately one minute.

2. Lower the heat to moderate-low and put in the coconut milk. Stirring continuously, cook until a thin film of oil develops on the surface.

3. Put in all of the rest of the ingredients except the eggplant. Bring to its boiling point, reduce heat, and simmer until the chicken starts to turn opaque, approximately five minutes.

4. Put in the eggplant and carry on cooking until the chicken is done to your preference, approximately 3 minutes more.

SIAMESE ROAST CHICKEN

Yield: Servings 2–4

INGREDIENTS:

- 1 clove garlic, minced
- 1 medium onion, chopped
- 1 tablespoon fish sauce
- 1 teaspoon (or to taste) dried red pepper flakes
- 1 whole roasting chicken
- 2 stalks lemongrass, thinly cut (soft inner core only)
- Salt and pepper to taste
- Vegetable oil

DIRECTIONS:

1. To prepare the marinade, put the lemongrass, onion, garlic, red pepper, and fish sauce in a food processor. Process until a thick paste is formed. Place in your fridge for minimum 30 minutes, overnight if possible.

2. Spread the marinade throughout the chicken cavity and then drizzle the cavity with salt and pepper. Rub the outside of the bird with a small amount of vegetable oil (or butter if you prefer) and sprinkle with salt and pepper. Put the bird in a roasting pan, and cover it using plastic wrap. Place in your fridge for a few hours to marinate, if possible. Take away the chicken from the fridge roughly thirty minutes before roasting.

3. Preheat your oven to 500 degrees. Take away the plastic wrap and put the bird in your oven, legs first, and roast for 50 to 60 minutes or until the juices run clear.

GRILLED EGGPLANT WITH AN ASIAN TWIST

Yield: Servings 4–6

INGREDIENTS:

- 4—8 Japanese eggplants (approximately 1½ pounds in all)
- Olive oil
- Salt and pepper to taste

DIRECTIONS:

1. Prepare a grill or broiler. Let it achieve high heat.
2. If the eggplants are relatively large, cut in half vertically. Toss them with a little olive oil just to coat, and sprinkle with salt and pepper. Put the eggplant either in a vegetable grilling basket or directly on the grill grate or broiler pan. Cook until soft, approximately fifteen to twenty minutes, turning midway through the cooking process.
3. Turn off the heat. Drizzle with lemon juice and fish sauce.
4. Decorate using basil leaves. Serve either hot or at room temperature.

JAPANESE EGGPLANT WITH TOFU

Yield: Servings 2–4

INGREDIENTS:

- 3 cups cut Japanese eggplant, approximately -inch thick
- ¼ pound extra-firm tofu, cut into little cubes
- 2–3 cloves garlic, finely chopped
- 4–6 tablespoons vegetable oil

DIRECTIONS:

1. Heat the oil in a big frying pan on moderate to high heat. Put in the garlic and sauté until it turns golden.

2. Put in the eggplant and tofu pieces; sauté, stirring continuously, for five to six minutes or until the eggplant is done to your preference.

3. Cautiously mix in the rest of the ingredients.

4. Serve instantly to avoid discoloration of the eggplant and basil.

PUMPKIN WITH PEPPERCORNS AND GARLIC

Yield: Servings 4–6

INGREDIENTS:

- 1 tablespoon vegetable oil

- 2 cloves garlic

- 2 cups fresh pumpkin pieces, cut into 1-inch cubes

- 30 peppercorns

DIRECTIONS:

1. Using a mortar and pestle, crush together the peppercorns and the garlic.

2. Put in the vegetable oil to a big sauté pan and heat on high. Put in the peppercorn-garlic mixture and stir-fry until the garlic just starts to brown.

3. Put in the pumpkin pieces, stirring to coat.

4. Put in the water and bring the water to a simmer. After the water has been reduced to half, mix in the fish sauce and sugar.

5. Continue to cook until the pumpkin is soft but not mushy.

6. Serve as a side dish.

SOUTHEASTERN VEGETABLE STEW

INGREDIENTS:

- ½ cup chopped cilantro

- 1 can straw mushrooms, drained

- 1 Chinese cabbage, cut into bite-sized pieces

- 1 cup cut leeks

- 1 tablespoon minced ginger

- 1 teaspoon vegetable oil

- 1 Western cabbage, quartered, cored, and slice into bitesized pieces

- 2 cups cut celery

- 2 tablespoons brown sugar

- 2 tablespoons dark soy sauce

- 3 cups bean noodles, soaked, and slice into short lengths

- 3 tablespoons chopped garlic

- 3 tablespoons fish sauce

- 4 cups roughly chopped kale

- 4 cups turnip, cut into bitesized pieces

- 5 cakes hard tofu, cut into bite-sized pieces

- 6 tablespoons soybean paste

- 8 cups vegetable stock

- Freshly ground pepper to taste

DIRECTIONS:

1. Bring the stock to its boiling point and put in the fish sauce, soy sauce, brown sugar.

2. Reduce the heat, put in the vegetables and tofu, and simmer vegetables are nearly soft.

3. In a small sauté pan, heat the oil on moderate heat. Put in paste and stir-fry until aromatic. Put in the garlic and ginger, until the garlic is golden.

4. Put in the soybean paste mixture to the soup. Mix in the noodles and cilantro, and simmer 5 more minutes.

5. Flavor it with the pepper and additional fish sauce to taste.

SPICY STIR-FRIED CORN

Yield: Servings 6–8

INGREDIENTS:

- 1 cup low-sodium vegetable broth

- 1 medium onion, minced

- 1 stalk lemongrass, minced (soft inner portion only)

- 1 tablespoon butter

- 2 tablespoons fish sauce Tabasco to taste

- 2 tablespoons lime juice

- 2 tablespoons vegetable oil

- 2 teaspoons lime zest

- 2 teaspoons minced garlic

- 4 cups corn kernels (fresh or frozen and thawed are best)

DIRECTIONS:

1. Put the oil in a big frying pan using high heat. Put in the lemongrass. Once it starts to brown, put in the garlic, butter, and onion. Continue to cook on high, letting the ingredients brown fairly.

2. Put in the corn kernels and cook until they brown. Mix in the vegetable stock; stirring continuously, cook the mixture for a couple of minutes, scraping the bottom of the pan to loosen any burned-on bits.

3. Mix in the rest of the ingredients and cook for 30 more seconds.

STIR–FRIED BLACK MUSHROOMS AND ASPARAGUS

Yield: Servings 4–6

INGREDIENTS:

- 1 ounce dried Chinese black mushrooms

- 1 pound asparagus spears, trimmed

- 1 tablespoon vegetable oil

- 1–2 cloves garlic, minced

- 3–4 tablespoons oyster sauce Tabasco (not necessary)

DIRECTIONS:

1. Put the dried mushrooms in a container and cover with hot water. Allow to soak for fifteen minutes. Drain, discard the stems, and slice into strips; set aside.

2. Heat the oil on moderate to high in a big frying pan. Put in the garlic and sauté until golden.

3. Mix in the mushrooms and carry on cooking, stirring continuously, for a minute.

4. Mix in the oyster sauce and a few drops of Tabasco if you wish.

5. Put in the asparagus spears. Sauté for two to 4 minutes or until the asparagus is done to your preference.

THAI PICKLED VEGETABLES

Yield: Approximately 6 cups

INGREDIENTS:

- ½ cup bok choy
- ½ cup cilantro leaves
- 1 big cucumber, seeded and slice into 3-inch-long, ½-inch wide strips
- 1 cup baby corn
- 1 cup broccoli florets
- 1 cup cut carrots
- 1 recipe Thai Vinegar Marinade
- 2–3 tablespoons toasted sesame seeds
- 4 cups water

DIRECTIONS:

1. Bring the water to its boiling point in a big pan. Put in the vegetables blanch for two to three minutes. Strain the vegetables and shock water to stop the cooking process.

2. Put the vegetables in a big container and pour the Thai Vinegar Marinade over the top. Allow to cool to room temperature and then place in your fridge for minimum 4 hours or maximum 2 weeks (yes, weeks).

3. Mix in the cilantro and sesame seeds just before you serve.

THAI VEGETABLE CURRY

Yield: Servings 4–6

INGREDIENTS:

- ¼ cup Green Curry
- ½ cup fresh minced cilantro
- 1 pound Japanese eggplant, cut into 1-inch slices
- 1 pound small boiling potatoes, quartered (or halved if large)
- 12 ounces baby carrots
- 2 cups broccoli florets
- 2 tablespoons vegetable oil
- 3 cups canned, unsweetened coconut milk
- 3 tablespoons fish sauce
- 3—4 ounces green beans, cut into 1-inch lengths

DIRECTIONS:

1. In a heavy stew pot, heat the oil. Put in the curry paste two to three minutes.
2. Put in the coconut milk and fish sauce; simmer for five minutes.
3. Put in the potatoes, eggplant, and carrots, and bring to a heat and simmer for about ten minutes. Put in the broccoli and carry on simmering until the vegetables are thoroughly cooked, ten minutes.
4. Just before you serve mix in the cilantro.

THAI–STYLE BEAN SPROUTS AND SNAP PEAS

Yield: Servings 4–6

INGREDIENTS:

- ½ pound sugar snap peas, trimmed
- 1 (1-inch) piece ginger, peeled and minced Pinch of white pepper
- 1 pound bean sprouts, washed meticulously and trimmed if required
- 1 small onion, thinly cut
- 1 tablespoon soy sauce
- 2 tablespoons vegetable oil

- Salt and sugar to taste

DIRECTIONS:

1. Heat the vegetable oil on moderate to high heat in a big frying pan.

2. Put in the onion and the ginger and sauté for a minute.

3. Mix in the white pepper and the soy sauce.

4. Put in the sugar snap peas and cook, stirring continuously, for a minute.

5. Put in the bean sprouts and cook for 1 more minute while stirring continuously.

6. Put in up to ½ teaspoon of salt and a big pinch of sugar to adjust the balance of the sauce. Serve instantly.

THAI-STYLE FRIED OKRA

Yield: Approximately 20

INGREDIENTS:

- ½ cup tapioca flour

- ½ cup water

- 1 cup all-purpose flour

- 1 cup vegetable oil

- 1 pound small okra, trimmed

- 1 recipe chili dipping sauce of your choice

- 1 teaspoon baking powder

DIRECTIONS:

1. In a moderate-sized-sized mixing container, mix the flours, the baking soda, and water to make a batter. Put in the okra pieces.

2. Heat the vegetable oil in a frying pan or wok using high heat. (It must be hot enough that a test piece of batter puffs up instantly.)

3. Put in the battered okra, a few at a time, and fry until golden.

4. Using a slotted spoon, remove the okra to paper towels to drain.

5. Serve hot with your favorite chili dipping sauce.

TROPICAL VEGETABLES

Yield: Servings 8–10

INGREDIENTS:

- ½ cup coconut milk
- 1 shallot, minced
- 1 tablespoon fish sauce
- 1 tablespoon Red Curry Paste (Page 17)
- 1 tablespoon sesame seeds
- 1 tablespoon Tamarind Concentrate (Page 20)
- 1 teaspoon vegetable oil
- 1 yellow or red bell pepper, seeded and julienned
- 2 cups bamboo shoots
- 2 cups bean sprouts
- 2 tablespoons brown sugar
- 2½ cups baby spinach leaves
- 2½ cups green beans, trimmed and slice into 1-inch lengths

DIRECTIONS:

1. To make the sauce, heat the vegetable oil in a small sauté pan on moderate to high. Put in the minced shallot and fry until golden. Move the fried shallot to paper towels to drain.

2. Using a mortar and pestle, crush half of the sesame seeds and half of the fried shallots together; set aside.

3. In a small deep cooking pan, mix the Red Curry Paste (Page 17) and the coconut milk, and bring to a simmer on moderate to low heat. Put in the tamarind, brown sugar, fish sauce, and the reserved sesame seed? shallot mixture. Decrease the heat to low and keep warm.

4. Bring a big deep cooking pan of water to its boiling point. Put in the green beans, the bell pepper pieces, and the bamboo shoots to the water and blanch for half a minute to one minute or until done to your preference. Using a slotted spoon, remove the vegetables from the water to a colander to drain.

5. Allow the water return to boiling and put in the spinach leaves and the bean sprouts. Instantly remove them from the water to drain.

6. Toss all of the vegetables together.

7. To serve, put the vegetables in the middle of a serving plate. Pour some of the sauce over the vegetables. Pass additional sauce separately.

VEGETABLES POACHED IN COCONUT MILK

INGREDIENTS:

- ½ cup cut mushrooms
- ½ cup long beans or green beans, broken into two-inch pieces
- ½ cup peas
- ½ teaspoon cut kaffir lime leaves
- 1 cup coconut milk
- 1 cup shredded cabbage
- 1 shallot, finely chopped
- 1 tablespoon brown sugar
- 1 tablespoon green peppercorns, tied together in a small pouch made from a Handi Wipe
- 1 tablespoon soy sauce
- 1 tablespoon Thai chilies, seeded and finely cut
- Rice, cooked in accordance with package directions

DIRECTIONS:

1. In a deep cooking pan bring the coconut milk to a gentle simmer moderate heat. Mix in the shallots, soy sauce, brown sugar, green peppercorn pouch, and lime leaves. Simmer for 1 until aromatic.
2. Put in the green beans, mushrooms, and cabbage, and return simmer. Cook for five to ten minutes or until soft.
3. Put in the peas and cook 1 more minute. Take away the pouch before you serve over rice.

VEGETARIAN STIR-FRY

Yield: Servings 4–6 as a main course

INGREDIENTS:

- ¼ cup asparagus tips
- ¼ cup bean sprouts
- ¼ cup bite-sized pieces bell pepper
- ¼ cup broccoli florets
- ¼ cup cauliflower florets
- ¼ cup cut mushrooms
- ¼ cup snow peas
- ¼ cup thinly cut celery
- ¼ cup water chestnuts
- 1 small onion, cut
- 1 tablespoon cornstarch, dissolved in a little water
- 1-2 tablespoons vegetable oil
- 2 cups bite-sized tofu pieces
- 2 tablespoons dark sweet soy sauce
- 2 tablespoons grated ginger
- 2 tablespoons minced garlic
- 4 tablespoons seeded and cut Thai chilies
- 4 tablespoons soy sauce
- Rice, cooked in accordance with package directions

DIRECTIONS:

1. Heat 1 tablespoon of oil in a big frying pan or wok over moderate-heat. Put in the tofu and sauté until a golden-brown colour is achieved. Move paper towels to drain.
2. Put in additional oil to the frying pan if required, and stir-fry the ginger, and chilies to release their fragrance, approximately 2 to Mix in the soy sauces and raise the heat to high.
3. Put in the reserved tofu and all the vegetables apart from the bean stir-fry for a minute.
4. Put in the cornstarch mixture and stir-fry for one more minute or until the vegetables are just thoroughly cooked and the sauce has thickened somewhat.
5. Put in the bean sprouts, stirring for a short period of time to warm them.
6. Serve over rice.

BROCCOLI NOODLES WITH GARLIC AND SOY

Yield: Servings 2–4

INGREDIENTS:

- 1 pound broccoli, trimmed into bite-sized florets
- 1 tablespoon sugar
- 1 tablespoon sweet soy sauce
- 1–2 tablespoons vegetable oil
- 16 ounces rice noodles
- 2 cloves garlic, minced
- 2 tablespoons soy sauce
- Fish sauce
- Hot sauce
- Lime wedges

DIRECTIONS:

1. Bring a pot of water to boil using high heat. Drop in the broccoli and blanch until soft-crisp or to your preference. Drain and save for later.
2. Soak the rice noodles in hot water until soft, approximately ten minutes.
3. In a big sauté pan, heat the vegetable oil on medium. Put in the garlic and stir-fry until golden. Put in the soy sauces and the sugar, stirring until the sugar has thoroughly blended.
4. Put in the reserved noodles, tossing until thoroughly coated with the sauce. Put in the broccoli and toss to coat.
5. Serve instantly with hot sauce, fish sauce, and lime wedges on the side.

CHIANG MAI CURRIED NOODLES

Yield: Servings 1–2

INGREDIENTS:

- ¼ pound ground pork

- ½ cup coconut milk

- 1 tablespoon chopped garlic

- 1 tablespoon curry powder Pinch of turmeric powder

- 1 tablespoon Red Curry Paste (Page 17)

- 1 teaspoon lime juice

- 2 tablespoons fish sauce Pinch of sugar

- 4 ounces rice noodles, soaked in water for twenty minutes to half an hour or until tender Lime wedges, for decoration

DIRECTIONS:

1. Heat the coconut milk in a wok or heavy frying pan on moderate heat. Mix in the curry paste and cook until aromatic and a thin film of oil separates out.

2. Put in the garlic and cook for approximately half a minute. Put in the remainingingredients apart from the pork, noodles, and limes, and cook until the sauce thickens slightly, stirring continuously.

3. Put in the pork and continue to stir until the meat is thoroughly cooked. Decrease the heat and keep the sauce warm.

4. Bring a pan of water to a rolling boil. Put the noodles in a wire basket or strainer and immerse the noodles in the water for ten to twenty seconds. Drain the noodles and move to serving plate.

5. Pour the sauce over the noodles. Serve with lime wedges.

CLEAR NOODLES WITH BAKED SHRIMP

Yield: Servings 2

INGREDIENTS:

- ¼ cup chopped cilantro

- 1 7-ounce package rice noodles

- 1 medium onion, thinly cut

- 1 tablespoon soy or fish sauce Sesame oil to taste

- 1 tablespoon vegetable oil

- 1 teaspoon sugar

- 2 cloves garlic, chopped
- 20–30 black peppercorns
- 6 big shrimp, shell on, washed and patted dry

DIRECTIONS:

1. Soak the noodles in hot water until soft, approximately ten minutes. Drain and save for later.

2. Using a mortar and pestle or a food processor, meticulously mix the garlic, cilantro, and peppercorns.

3. Put in the vegetable oil to a wok or big frying pan using low heat. Put in the garlic mixture and stir-fry for a minute. Put in the cut onion and carry on cooking until the onion is soft, then remove the heat.

4. Put in the sugar, soy sauce, and a few drops of sesame oil to the wok; stir until blended. Put in the noodles and toss to coat. Pour the noodle mixture into an ovenproof baking dish. Put the whole shrimp on top of the noodles, cover the dish, and bake for about twenty minutes in a 400-degree oven. Serve instantly.

CURRIED RICE NOODLES WITH TOFU AND EGG

INGREDIENTS:

- ½ of a 7-ounce package rice noodles
- ½ teaspoon ground coriander
- ½ teaspoon ground cumin
- 1 cup bean sprouts
- 1 cup coconut milk
- 1 cup cubed extra-firm tofu
- 1 green onion, trimmed and thinly cut
- 1 hard-boiled egg, cut
- 1 tablespoon Red Curry Paste (Page 17)
- 1 teaspoon curry powder
- 2 tablespoons chopped cilantro
- 2 tablespoons fish sauce

- 2 tablespoons minced shallots
- 2 tablespoons sugar
- 2–3 cups water

DIRECTIONS:

1. In a small container, meticulously mix the coriander, cumin, curry powder, and curry paste.
2. Pour the coconut milk into a moderate-sized deep cooking pan. Mix in the curry paste mixture and place on moderate heat. Heat to a simmer and cook for approximately five minutes or until a slim layer of yellow oil starts to make on the surface of the sauce.
3. Mix in 2 cups of the water, the shallots, sugar, and fish sauce. Return the sauce to a simmer and allow to cook thirty minutes, stirring once in a while and putting in extra water if required.
4. In the meantime, soak the noodles in hot water for about ten minutes or until tender.
5. To serve, mound the noodles into serving bowls. Top the noodles with the cut egg, tofu, and bean sprouts. Ladle some of the curry sauce over top. Drizzle with green onion slices and chopped cilantro.

FIRE NOODLES

Yield: Servings 4–6

INGREDIENTS:

- fifteen–20 (or to taste) Thai bird chilies, stemmed and seeded
- 1 pound presliced fresh rice noodles (available at Asian grocery stores and on the Internet)
- 2 tablespoons vegetable oil
- 2 whole boneless, skinless chicken breasts, cut into bite-sized pieces
- 2 tablespoons fish sauce
- 2 tablespoons sweet black soy sauce
- 1 tablespoon oyster sauce
- 1 teaspoon white pepper
- 1½ tablespoons sugar
- 1 (8-ounce) can bamboo shoots, drained
- 1½ cups loose-packed basil and/or mint
- 5–10 (or to taste) cloves garlic

DIRECTIONS:

1. Put the chilies and garlic cloves in a food processor and pulse until meticulously mashed together; set aside.

2. Bring a kettle of water to its boiling point. Put the noodles in a big colander and pour the hot water over them. Cautiously unfold and separate the noodles; set aside.

3. Heat the oil in a wok or big frying pan on moderate to high heat. When it is fairly hot, cautiously put in the reserved chili-garlic mixture and stir-fry for fifteen seconds to release the aromas.

4. Increase the heat to high, put in the chicken, and stir-fry until it starts to lose its color, approximately half a minute.

5. Mix in the fish sauce, soy sauce, oyster sauce, white pepper, and sugar.

6. Put in the noodles and continue to stir-fry for half a minute, tossing them with the other ingredients.

7. Put in the bamboo shoots and cook for one more minute.

8. Remove the heat and put in the basil.

FLOWERED LIME NOODLES

Yield: Servings 4

INGREDIENTS:

- 1 tablespoon salted butter
- 2–3 tablespoons lime juice
- 4 ounces grated Parmesan cheese
- 8 ounces angel hair pasta
- Black pepper
- Lime slices
- Rose petals or other organic edible flowers

DIRECTIONS:

1. Bring a big pot of water to its boiling point using high heat. Put in pasta and cook in accordance with package instructions; drain.

2. Toss the pasta with butter, lime juice, and parmesan.

3. To serve, top with rose or flower petals and lime slices. Pass black pepper at the table.

PAD THAI

Yield: Servings 2–4

INGREDIENTS:

- ¼ cup brown sugar
- ¼ cup chopped chives
- ¼ cup fish sauce
- ½ cup chopped roasted peanuts
- ½ cup cooked salad shrimp
- 1 cup bean sprouts
- 1 medium egg, beaten
- 2 tablespoons chopped shallots
- 2 tablespoons vegetable oil
- 5–6 cloves garlic, finely chopped
- 6–8 teaspoons Tamarind Concentrate (Page 20)
- 8 ounces rice noodles

Garnish:

- ½ cup bean sprouts
- ½ cup chopped chives
- ½ cup crudely ground roasted peanuts
- 1 lime cut into wedges
- 1 tablespoon fish sauce
- 1 tablespoon lime juice
- 1 tablespoon Tamarind Concentrate (Page 20)

DIRECTIONS:

1. Soak the noodles in water at room temperature for thirty minutes or until tender. Drain and save for later.

2. Heat the vegetable oil in a wok or frying pan on moderate to high heat. Put in the garlic and shallots, and for a short period of time stir-fry until they start to change color.

3. Put in the reserved noodles and all the rest of the ingredients except the egg and the bean sprouts, and stir-fry until hot.

4. While continuously stirring, slowly sprinkle in the beaten egg.

5. Put in the bean sprouts and cook for no more than another half a minute.

6. In a small container combine all of the decorate ingredients apart from the lime wedges.

7. To serve, position the Pad Thai on a serving platter. Top with the decorate and surround with lime wedges.

PANANG MUSSELS AND NOODLES

Yield: Servings 4

INGREDIENTS:

* ¼ cup white wine

* 1 medium onion, chopped

* 1 pound Asian egg noodles

* 1 pound mussels, washed and debearded

* 1 teaspoon Black Bean Paste (Page 10)

* 2 cups chicken broth

* 2 tablespoons vegetable oil

* 6—8 stalks celery, chopped

DIRECTIONS:

1. Bring a big pot of water to its boiling point using high heat. Put in the noodles and cook until firm to the bite. Wash the noodles under cold water and save for later.

2. Heat the oil in a big sauté pan on moderate heat. Put in the Black Bean Paste, onion, and celery, and sauté for five minutes.

3. Put in the wine and chicken broth, and bring to its boiling point.

4. Put in the mussels and decrease the heat to low; cover and steam for five minutes.

5. To serve, split the noodles between 4 soup plates. Split the mussels between the plates (discarding any that have not opened) and pour the broth over the top.

PAN–FRIED NOODLES

Yield: Servings 6–8

INGREDIENTS:

- ¼ cup minced chives
- ¾ pound fresh lo mein noodles or angel hair pasta
- 2 tablespoons (or to taste) prepared chili-garlic paste
- 3 tablespoons vegetable oil, divided
- Salt to taste

DIRECTIONS:

1. Boil the noodles in a big pot for no more than two to three minutes. Drain, wash under cold water, and drain once more.
2. Put in the chives, chili paste, 1 tablespoon of the oil, and salt to the noodles; toss to coat, and tweak seasonings.
3. In a heavy-bottomed 10-inch frying pan, heat the rest of the oil on moderate to high heat. When it is hot, put in the noodle mixture, spreading uniformly. Push the noodles into the pan using the back of a spatula. Cook for roughly two minutes. Decrease the heat and carry on cooking until the noodles are well browned. Flip the noodles over in 1 piece. Carry on cooking until browned, putting in additional oil if required.
4. To serve, chop the noodles into wedges.

POACHED CHICKEN BREAST WITH PEANUT SAUCE AND NOODLES

Yield: Servings 6

INGREDIENTS:

- ¼ cup chicken stock
- ¼ cup lime juice
- ¼cup half-and-half
- 1 cup crispy peanut butter
- 1 pound Chinese egg noodles (mein)

- 1 pound snow peas, trimmed and blanched
- 1 tablespoon peanut oil
- 1 tablespoon sesame oil
- 1½ cups coconut milk
- 2 tablespoons fish sauce
- 2 teaspoons brown sugar
- 3 whole boneless, skinless chicken breasts, halved and poached
- 4 cloves garlic, minced
- 6–8 green onions, trimmed and thinly cut
- Salt and pepper to taste

DIRECTIONS:

1. Mix the peanut butter, coconut milk, fish sauce, lime juice, brown sugar, garlic, salt, and pepper in a small deep cooking pan using low heat. Cook until the desired smoothness is achieved and thick, stirring regularly.
2. Move to a blender and purée.
3. Put in the chicken stock and half-and-half, and blend; set aside.
4. Bring a big pot of water to its boiling point. Put in the noodles and cook until firm to the bite. Drain, wash under cold water, and drain once more.
5. Toss the noodles with the peanut and sesame oils.
6. To serve, place some pasta in the center of each serving plate. Ladle some of the peanut sauce over the pasta. Slice each chicken breast on the diagonal. Move 1 cut breast to the top of each portion of noodles. Ladle some additional peanut sauce over the chicken. Surround the noodles with the snow peas. Decorate using the cut green onions.

RICE STICK NOODLES WITH CHICKEN AND VEGETABLES

Yield: Servings 2–4

INGREDIENTS:

Noodles:

- 1 tablespoon sweet black soy sauce
- 2 tablespoons vegetable oil
- 8 ounces rice stick noodles

Chicken and vegetables:

- ¼ cup chicken broth
- ¼– cup cut green onions
- ¼ pound broccoli, chopped
- ½ teaspoon Tabasco
- 1 big whole boneless, skinless chicken breast, cut into bite-sized strips
- 1 cup bean sprouts
- 1 small onion, finely cut
- 1 small red bell pepper, seeded and slice into strips
- 1 tablespoon cornstarch mixed with
- 1 tablespoon water
- 1¼ cups cut Japanese eggplant
- 2 tablespoons fish sauce
- 2 tablespoons vegetable oil
- 2 tablespoons Yellow Bean Sauce (Page 24)
- 3 tablespoons brown sugar
- 4 cloves garlic, chopped

NOODLES:

1. Soak the noodles in warm water for fifteen minutes or until soft; drain.
2. Put a wok on moderate to high heat and put in the vegetable oil. Once the oil is hot, put in the noodles and stir-fry vigorously until they are thoroughly heated, approximately 45 seconds to one minute.
3. Put in the soy sauce and continue to stir-fry for 1 more minute.
4. Put the noodles on a serving platter, covered in foil, in a warm oven until ready to serve.

CHICKEN AND VEGETABLES:

1. Put a wok on moderate to high heat and put in the vegetable oil. Once the oil is hot, put in the garlic and stir-fry for a short period of time to release its aroma.

2. Put in the chicken and cook until it begins to become opaque.

3. Put in the broccoli and stir-fry for half a minute.

4. Put in the onion and eggplant and stir-fry for a couple of minutes.

5. Put in the Tabasco, fish sauce, yellow bean sauce, and sugar. Stir-fry for a minute.

6. Put in the broth, cornstarch mixture, bean sprouts, green onions, and red bell pepper; cook until vegetables are soft-crisp.

7. To serve, ladle the chicken and vegetable mixture over the reserved noodles.

SESAME NOODLES WITH VEGGIES

Yield: Servings 2–4

INGREDIENTS:

- 1 red bell pepper, seeded and slice into strips
- 1 tablespoon sesame oil
- 2 cloves garlic, minced
- 2 cups broccoli, cut into bite-sized pieces
- 2 tablespoons vegetable oil
- 2 tablespoons water
- 2–3 tablespoons prepared chili sauce
- 2–3 tablespoons soy sauce
- 3 tablespoons sesame seeds
- 4 ounces tofu, cut into bitesized cubes
- 8 ounces egg noodles

DIRECTIONS:

1. Heat the oil in a big Sauté pan or wok on moderate heat. Put in the garlic and sauté until golden, roughly two minutes.

2. Put in the broccoli and red bell pepper, and stir-fry for two to three minutes. Put in the water, cover, and let the vegetables steam until soft, roughly five minutes.

3. Bring a big pot of water to boil. Put in the noodles and cook until firm to the bite; drain.

4. While the noodles are cooking, put in the rest of the ingredients to the broccoli mixture. Turn off the heat, put in the noodles, and toss to blend.

SPICY EGG NOODLES WITH SLICED PORK

INGREDIENTS:

- ½ teaspoon vegetable oil
- 1 cup bean sprouts
- 1 package fresh angel hair pasta
- 1 small Barbecued Pork
- 1 small cabbage, shredded
- 2 scallions, trimmed and thinly cut
- 2 tablespoons fish sauce
- 2 tablespoons sugar
- 2 teaspoons chopped cilantro
- 2 teaspoons ground dried red chili pepper (or to taste)
- 4 tablespoons minced garlic
- 4–6 tablespoons rice vinegar
- Freshly ground black pepper to taste
- Tenderloin , thinly cut

DIRECTIONS:

1. Bring a big pot of water to its boiling point using high heat. Put in the cabbage and blanch about half a minute. Using a slotted spoon, remove the cabbage from the boiling water; set aside.
2. Allow the water return to boiling. Put in the bean sprouts and blanch for ten seconds. Using a slotted spoon, remove the sprouts from the water; set aside.
3. Return the water to boiling. Put in the fresh angel hair pasta and cook in accordance with package directions. Drain the pasta and place it in a big mixing container.
4. In a small sauté pan, heat the vegetable oil on moderate heat. Put in the garlic and sauté until golden. Turn off the heat. Mix in the fish sauce, sugar, rice vinegar, and dried chili pepper.
5. Pour the sauce over the pasta and toss to coat.

6. To serve, split the cabbage and the bean sprouts into 2 to 4 portions and place in the middle of serving plates. Split the noodles into 2 to 4 portions and place over the cabbage and sprouts. Split the pork slices over the noodles. Grind black pepper to taste over the noodles and top with the cut scallions and chopped cilantro.

THAI NOODLES WITH CHICKEN AND PORK

Yield: Servings 4–6

INGREDIENTS:

For the sauce:

- ¼ teaspoon white pepper
- ½ cup peanut butter
- ½ cup soy sauce
- 1 teaspoon hot chili oil
- 1 teaspoon minced garlic
- 3 tablespoons honey
- 3 tablespoons sesame oil

For the noodles:

- ½ pound boneless pork tenderloin, cut into fine strips
- ½ pound boneless, skinless chicken breast, cut thin
- ½ teaspoon minced garlic
- 1 big yellow onion, diced
- 1 pound dry flat Asian noodles
- 1 tablespoon vegetable oil
- 1 teaspoon sesame oil
- 6 ounces salad shrimp
- 6–8 green onions, trimmed, white portions cut, green portions julienned

DIRECTIONS:

1. Put all of the sauce ingredients in a blender and pulse until smooth; set aside.

2. Bring a big pot of water to boil using high heat. Prepare the noodles in accordance with package directions, drain, and mix in the sauce mixture, saving for later ¼ cup; set aside.

3. Heat the oils in a big sautée pan using high heat. Put in the garlic and sautée for a short period of time.

4. Put in the chicken, pork, and onion, and sauté for five to six minutes or until the meats are thoroughly cooked.

5. Put in the white portion of the green onion and the shrimp and sautée for two more minutes.

6. Put in the green parts of the onions and the rest of the sauce, stirring until everything is thoroughly coated.

7. To serve, put the noodles on a big platter and top with the meat sautée. Pass additional hot chili oil separately.

BASIC STICKY RICE

Yield: Servings 2–4

INGREDIENTS:

- 1 cup glutinous rice
- Water

DIRECTIONS:

1. Put the rice in a container, completely cover it with water, and allow to soak overnight. Drain before you use.

2. Coat a steamer basket or colander with moistened cheesecloth. (This prevents the grains of rice from falling through the holes in the colander.)

3. Spread the rice over the cheesecloth as uniformly as you can.

4. Bring a pan of water with a cover to a rolling boil. Put the basket over the boiling water, ensuring that the bottom of it doesn't come in contact with the water. Cover firmly and allow to steam for about twenty-five minutes.

BASIC WHITE RICE

Yield: Servings 2–4

INGREDIENTS:

- 1 cup long-grain rice (such as Jasmine)
- 2 cups water

DIRECTIONS:

1. Put the rice in a colander and run under cool water.
2. Put the rice and the water in a moderate-sized pot. Stir for a short period of time. Bring to a rolling boil on moderate to high heat. Decrease the heat to low, cover, and simmer for eighteen to twenty minutes.
3. Take away the rice from the heat, keeping it covered, and allow it to rest for minimum ten minutes.
4. Fluff the rice just before you serve.

CHICKEN FRIED RICE

Yield: Servings 4–6

INGREDIENTS:

- ¼ cup chicken stock
- ¼ cup dry sherry
- ¼ cup fish sauce
- ½ medium head Chinese cabbage, crudely chopped
- 1 cup shredded, cooked chicken
- 1 cup snow peas, trimmed and slice into bite-sized pieces
- 1 medium onion, cut
- 1 tablespoon minced garlic
- 1 tablespoon minced ginger
- 1 tablespoon vegetable oil
- 2 eggs, beaten
- 3 cups cooked long-grain white rice

DIRECTIONS:

1. In a big frying pan or wok, heat the oil on moderate to low heat. Put in the garlic, ginger, and onion, and stir-fry for five minutes or until the onion becomes translucent.
2. Put in the cabbage, raise the heat to moderate, and stir-fry for about ten minutes.

3. Put in the rice and stir-fry for a couple of minutes.

4. Mix the fish sauce, sherry, and stock in a small container; put in to the wok and stir until blended.

5. Put in the snow peas and chicken; stir-fry for a couple of minutes more.

6. Move the rice to the sides of the wok, making a hole in the center. Pour the eggs into the hole and cook for approximately 1 minute, stirring the eggs using a fork. Fold the cooked eggs into the fried rice.

CURRIED RICE

Yield: Servings 4–6

INGREDIENTS:

- ¼ cup golden raisins (regular raisins can be substituted)
- ½ cup finely chopped onion
- 1 teaspoon curry powder
- 1½ cups long-grained rice
- 2 tablespoons vegetable oil
- 2 teaspoons Mango Chutney (Page 220)
- 2¾ cups vegetable stock
- Salt to taste

DIRECTIONS:

1. In a moderate-sized-sized pot, heat the oil on moderate heat. Put in the onions and sautée. for a couple of minutes, until the onions are tender but not browned.

2. Put in the rice and continue to sautée. for another two minutes. Put in the curry powder and sauté for 1 more minute.

3. Pour in the vegetable stock and sprinkle with salt. Bring to its boiling point, then decrease the heat and cover. Simmer the rice for fifteen to twenty minutes, stirring once in a while.

4. Put in the raisins and the chutney. Continue to simmer for another five minutes or until soft.

PEANUT DIPPING SAUCE — 3

Yield: Approximately 2 cups

INGREDIENTS:

- ½ cup smooth peanut butter

- 1 cup canned coconut milk

- 1 tablespoon fish sauce

- 1 teaspoon fresh lemon juice

- 1 teaspoon Tabasco

- 2 tablespoons fresh lime juice

- 2 teaspoons light brown sugar

- 2 teaspoons soy sauce

- 3 shallots

DIRECTIONS:

1. Roast the shallots in an oven preheated to 325 degrees for approximately five minutes or until tender. Allow them to cool to roughly room temperature.

2. Put all ingredients in a blender or food processor and pulse until the desired smoothness is achieved.

PEANUT PESTO

Yield: Approximately 2 cups

INGREDIENTS:

- ¼ cup honey

- ¼ teaspoon (or to taste) red pepper flakes

- ½ cup sesame oil

- ½ cup soy sauce

- 1 cup unsalted roasted peanuts

- 2–3 cloves garlic, minced

- 1 cup water

DIRECTIONS:

1. Put the peanuts in a food processor fitted using a metal blade; pulse until fine.

2. While continuing to blend, put in the rest of the ingredients one by one through the feed tube until well mixed.

QUICK HOT DIPPING SAUCE

Yield: Approximately ½ cup

INGREDIENTS:

- ½ cup white vinegar
- 1 loaded tablespoon prepared chili-garlic sauce

DIRECTIONS:

1. Mix the 2 ingredients before you serve.

SPICY THAI DRESSING

Yield: Approximately 1 cup

INGREDIENTS:

- 1 fresh red cayenne pepper or
- 1 tablespoon plus 1 teaspoon rice wine vinegar
- 1 tablespoon sesame oil
- 1 teaspoon grated gingerroot
- 1 teaspoon sugar
- 2 cloves garlic
- 2 tablespoons soy sauce
- 2 Thai peppers, stemmed, seeded, and slice into pieces
- 3 tablespoons water

DIRECTIONS:

1. Put all the ingredients in a blender and process until the desired smoothness is achieved.

SWEET-AND-SOUR DIPPING SAUCE

Yield: Approximately 1½ cups

INGREDIENTS:

- ½ cup white vinegar
- ½ teaspoon salt

- 1 cup sugar
- 1 loaded tablespoon prepared chili-garlic sauce

DIRECTIONS:

1. Mix the vinegar, sugar, and salt in a small deep cooking pan on moderate to high heat; bring to its boiling point, reduce to a simmer, and cook for eight to ten minutes, stirring once in a while.
2. Mix in the chili sauce and turn off the heat. Allow to cool to room temperature before you serve.

THAI-STYLE PLUM DIPPING SAUCE

Yield: Approximately 2 cups

INGREDIENTS:

- 2 tablespoons honey Tabasco to taste
- 1 cup plum preserves
- 1 cup water
- 1 cup white vinegar

DIRECTIONS:

1. Put all the ingredients apart from the Tabasco in a food processor or blender, and process until the desired smoothness is achieved.
2. Move the mixture to a small deep cooking pan and bring to its boiling point on moderate heat; decrease the heat and simmer until thick, approximately twelve to fifteen minutes.
3. Allow to cool completely, then mix in the Tabasco.

3-FLAVOR RICE STICKS

Yield: Servings 4–6

INGREDIENTS:

- 1 pound rice sticks, broken into 3-inch segments
- Cayenne pepper to taste
- Curry powder to taste
- Salt to taste
- Vegetable oil for frying

DIRECTIONS:

1. Pour 2 to 3 inches of vegetable oil into a big frying pan and heat to 350 degrees. Fry the rice sticks in batches (ensuring not to overcrowd the pan), turning them swiftly as they puff up. After they stop crackling in the oil, move the puffed sticks to paper towels to drain.

2. While the rice sticks are still hot, drizzle salt on 1 batch; drizzle a second batch with curry powder; and a third batch with cayenne pepper to taste.

BASIL AND SHRIMP WEDGES

Yield: Servings 4–6 as an appetizer or 2 as a brunch item

INGREDIENTS:

- ½ cup julienned basil
- ½ pound cooked salad shrimp
- 1 green onion, trimmed and thinly cut
- 1 teaspoon fish sauce
- 1½ teaspoons vegetable oil, divided
- 2 tablespoons water
- 4 eggs
- Salt and pepper to taste

DIRECTIONS:

1. Put 1 teaspoon of the vegetable oil in a sauté pan on moderate heat. Put in the shrimp and green onion, and sauté until the shrimp are warmed through, roughly two minutes. Put in the basil and fish sauce and cook for 1 more minute. Set aside.

2. In a big container, whisk together the eggs, water, and salt and pepper, then mix in the shrimp mixture.

3. Put the remaining ½ teaspoon of vegetable oil in an omelet pan on moderate heat. Put in the egg mixture and cook until the omelet starts to brown. Turn over the omelet and carry on cooking until set.

4. To serve, slide the omelet onto a serving plate and cut it into wedges. Serve with a Thai dipping sauce of your choice.

CHICKEN, SHRIMP, AND BEEF SATAY

Yield: 4–6 chicken skewers or 6–8 shrimp or beef skewers

Chicken

- 1 recipe Peanut Dipping Sauce
- 1 recipe Thai Marinade (Page 22)
- 3 whole boneless, skinless chicken breasts, cut into lengthy strips about ½-inch wide

DIRECTIONS:

1. Thread the chicken strips onto presoaked bamboo skewers or onto metal skewers. Put the skewers in a flat pan and cover with marinade. Marinate the chicken in your fridge overnight.
2. Cook the skewers on the grill or under the broiler, coating and turning them until they are thoroughly cooked, approximately six to eight minutes.
3. Serve with the peanut sauce for dipping.

Shrimp

- 1 recipe Peanut Dipping Sauce
- 1 recipe Thai Marinade (Page 22)
- 24 big shrimp, shelled and deveined

DIRECTIONS:

1. Thread the shrimp onto presoaked bamboo skewers or onto metal skewers (about 3 shrimp per skewer). Put the skewers in a flat pan and cover with marinade. Marinate the shrimp for minimum fifteen minutes, but no longer than an hour.
2. Cook the skewers on the grill or under the broiler, coating and turning them frequently until just opaque, approximately three to four minutes.
3. Serve with the peanut sauce for dipping.

Beef

- 1 recipe Thai Marinade (Page 22)
- 1 recipe Peanut Dipping Sauce
- 1-1½ pounds sirloin steak, fat and sinew removed, cut into ½-inch-wide strips

DIRECTIONS:

1. Thread the beef strips onto presoaked bamboo skewers or onto metal skewers. Put the skewers in a flat pan and cover with marinade. Marinate the beef in your fridge overnight.

2. Cook the skewers on the grill or under the broiler, coating and turning them frequently until done to your preference, approximately six to eight minutes for medium.

3. Serve with the peanut sauce for dipping.

CHINESE-STYLE DUMPLINGS

Yield: 15–20 dumplings

INGREDIENTS:

- ¼ cup sticky rice flour
- ¼ cup tapioca flour
- ½ cup water
- 1 cup rice flour
- 1 tablespoon soy sauce
- 1 teaspoon vegetable oil
- 2 cups chives, cut into ½–inch lengths

DIRECTIONS:

1. In a moderate-sized-sized deep cooking pan, mix together the sticky rice flour, the rice flour, and the water. Turn the heat to moderate and cook, stirring continuously until the mixture has the consistency of glue. (If the mixture becomes too sticky, decrease the heat to low.) Take away the batter from the heat and swiftly mix in the tapioca flour. Set aside to cool completely.

2. In the meantime, put in the vegetable oil to a frying pan big enough to easily hold the chives, and heat on high. Put in the chives and the soy sauce. Stir-fry the chives just until they wilt. Be careful not to let the chives cook excessively. Turn off the heat and save for later.

3. Once the dough has reached room temperature, check its consistency. If it is too sticky to work with, add a little extra tapioca flour.

4. To make the dumplings, roll the batter into balls an inch in diameter. Using your fingers, flatten each ball into a disk approximately four inches across. Ladle approximately 1 tablespoon of the chives into the middle of each disk. Fold the disk in half and pinch the edges together to make a halfmoon-shaped packet.

5. Put the dumplings in a prepared steamer for five to 8 minutes or until the dough is cooked. Serve with a spicy dipping sauce of your choice.

COLD SESAME NOODLES

Yield: Servings 2–4

INGREDIENTS:

- ¼ cup creamy peanut butter or tahini
- ¼–½ teaspoon dried red pepper flakes
- 1 pound angel hair pasta
- 1 tablespoon grated ginger
- 1–2 green onions, trimmed and thinly cut (not necessary)
- 2 tablespoons rice vinegar
- 2 tablespoons sesame oil

DIRECTIONS:

1. Cook the pasta in accordance with package directions. Wash under cold water, then set aside.
2. Vigorously whisk together the rest of the ingredients; pour over pasta, tossing to coat.
3. Decorate using green onion if you wish.

CRAB SPRING ROLLS

Yield: fifteen rolls

INGREDIENTS:

- ¼–½ teaspoon grated lime peel
- 1 pound crabmeat, picked over to remove any shells, and shredded
- 1 tablespoon mayonnaise
- 2 egg yolks, lightly beaten
- Canola oil for deep frying
- fifteen small, soft Boston lettuce leaves
- fifteen spring roll or egg roll wrappers
- Mint leaves
- Parsley leaves

DIRECTIONS:

1. In a small container, combine the crabmeat with the mayonnaise and lime peel.

2. Put 1 tablespoon of the crabmeat mixture in the middle of 1 spring roll wrapper. Fold a pointed end of the wrapper over the crabmeat, then fold the opposite point over the top of the folded point. Brush a small amount of the egg yolk over the top of the uncovered wrapper, then fold the bottom point over the crabmeat and roll to make a tight packet; set aside. Repeat with the rest of the crabmeat and wrappers.

3. Heat the oil to 365 degrees in a frying pan or deep fryer. Deep-fry the rolls three to 4 at a time for a couple of minutes or so, until they are a golden brown; drain using paper towels.

4. To serve, wrap each spring roll in a wrapper with a single piece of lettuce, and a drizzling of mint and parsley. Serve with a dipping sauce of your choice.

FRAGRANT WHITE RICE

Yield: Servings 6–8

INGREDIENTS:

- 1 stalk lemongrass, cut into thin rings (inner soft potion only)
- 10 fresh curry leaves
- 1¼ cups coconut milk
- 1¾ cups water
- 2 mace blades
- 2 tablespoons vegetable oil
- 2½ cups Jasmine rice
- 6 cloves
- Salt and freshly ground pepper to taste
- Zest of ½ kaffir lime

DIRECTIONS:

1. In a moderate-sized-large deep cooking pan, heat the oil on medium. Put in the curry leaves and sautée. until you can start to smell the aroma. Put in the lime zest and the rest of the spices and sautée. for another two to three minutes, stirring continuously.

2. Put in the rice to the pot and stir until blended with the spice mixture. Put in the water, coconut milk, and salt and pepper. Bring to its boiling point; reduce heat, cover, and simmer for fifteen to twenty minutes or until the liquids have been absorbed. Adjust seasoning.

BASIL SCALLOPS

Yield: Servings 2–4

INGREDIENTS:

- ¼ cup shredded bamboo shoots
- ½ pound bay scallops, cleaned
- 1 (14-ounce) can straw mushrooms, drained
- 2 tablespoons vegetable oil
- 3 cloves garlic, chopped
- 3 kaffir lime leaves, julienned, or the peel of 1 small lime cut into fine strips
- 3 tablespoons oyster sauce
- fifteen–20 fresh basil leaves

DIRECTIONS:

1. In a wok or frying pan, heat the oil on high. Put in the garlic and lime leaves, and stir-fry until aromatic, approximately fifteen seconds.
2. Put in the scallops, mushrooms, bamboo shoots, and oyster sauce; continue to stir-fry for roughly four to five minutes or until the scallops are done to your preference.
3. Stir in the basil leaves and serve instantly.

BROILED SALMON WITH 5-SPICE LIME BUTTER

Yield: Servings 2

INGREDIENTS:

- ¼–½ teaspoon Chinese 5-spice powder
- 1 tablespoon unsalted butter
- 2 (6-ounce) salmon fillets, washed and patted dry
- 2 teaspoons lime juice
- Vegetable oil

DIRECTIONS:

1. Using paper towels, wipe a thin coat of vegetable oil over a broiler pan.
2. Preheat your broiler on high, with the rack set on the upper third of the oven.
3. Melt the butter using low heat in a small deep cooking pan. Mix in the 5-spice powder and lime juice; keep warm.
4. Put the salmon on the broiler pan, skin side up. Broil for two to 4 minutes or until the skin is crunchy. Turn the salmon over and broil two minutes more or until done to your preference.
5. Move the salmon to 2 plates and spoon the butter sauce over the top.

CLAMS WITH HOT BASIL

Yield: Servings 4–6

INGREDIENTS:

- 1 bunch basil (Thai variety preferred), trimmed and julienned
- 1 tablespoon vegetable oil
- 2 cloves garlic
- 2 pounds Manila clams, cleaned
- 2 small dried red chili peppers, crushed
- 2 teaspoons sugar
- 4 teaspoons fish sauce

DIRECTIONS:

1. Heat the oil in a big frying pan on high. Put in the chili peppers, garlic, and clams. Mix the clams until they open, approximately 4 to five minutes. Discard any clams that stay closed.
2. Put in the fish sauce and sugar; stir until well blended.
3. Put in the basil and stir until it wilts.
4. Serve instantly either as an appetizer or with rice as a main course.

CURRIED MUSSELS

Yield: Servings 2–4

INGREDIENTS:

- ½ cup sour cream

- ½ cup sweet white wine, such as Riesling

- 1 tablespoon lemon juice

- 1 teaspoon (or to taste) curry powder

- 2 pounds mussels, debearded and washed well

- 2 shallots, minced

- 2 tablespoons butter

DIRECTIONS:

1. In a pan big enough to hold all of the mussels, melt the butter on moderate heat. Put in the shallots and sauté until tender and translucent.

2. Put in the wine and the mussels and raise the heat to high. Cover and cook, shaking the pan once in a while, until the mussels open, roughly ten minutes.

3. Take away the mussels from the pan, discarding any mussels that haven't opened. Strain the pan liquid through a strainer and return it to the pan. Bring to its boiling point, then mix in the sour cream and curry powder.

4. Lower the heat to moderate-low and put in the lemon juice. Cook for two to three minutes. Tweak the seasonings of the sauce if required with salt and curry powder.

5. Return the mussels to the broth, coating them. Reheat before you serve.

CURRIED SHRIMP WITH PEAS

Yield: Servings 4–6

INGREDIENTS:

- 1 (10-ounce) package thawed frozen peas

- 1 (14-ounce) can unsweetened coconut milk

- 1 cup packed basil leaves, chopped

- 1 cup packed cilantro, chopped

- 1 tablespoon vegetable oil

- 1½ teaspoons Red Curry Paste (Page 17)

- 2 pounds big shrimp, peeled and deveined

- 2–3 teaspoons brown sugar
- 4 teaspoons fish sauce
- Jasmine rice, cooked in accordance with package directions

DIRECTIONS:

1. In a big pot, mix the curry paste, vegetable oil, and ¼ cup of the coconut milk; cook on moderate heat for one to two minutes.
2. Mix in the rest of the coconut milk and cook for an extra five minutes.
3. Put in the fish sauce and sugar, and cook for a minute more.
4. Put in the shrimp, basil, and cilantro; decrease the heat slightly and cook for four to five minutes or until the shrimp are almost done.
5. Put in the peas and cook two minutes more.
6. Serve over Jasmine rice.